Supplemental Copyright Information

Library of Congress Copyright Office

Supplemental Copyright Information

As Published by The United States Copyright Office (USCO)

Included in this Project Gutenberg etext are the following items, published by the United States Copyright Office. Each item is separated by a page break and a string of 5 asterisks (*****).

a. Circular 3: Copyright Notice b. Circular 15: Renewal of Copyright c. Circular 15t: Extension of Copyright Terms d. Circular 22: Highlights of Copyright Amendments Contained in the Uruguay Round Agreements Act (URAA) e. WIPO Copyright Treaty

*****

United States Copyright Office

Circular 3

Copyright Notice

==

INTRODUCTION

The use of a copyright notice is no longer required under U.S. law, although it is often beneficial. Because prior law did contain such a requirement, however, the use of notice is still relevant to the copyright status of older works.

This circular discusses both the copyright notice provisions as originally enacted in the 1976 Copyright Act (title 17, U.S. Code), which took effect January 1, 1978, and the effect of the 1988 Berne Convention Implementation Act, which amended the copyright law to make the use of a copyright notice optional on copies of *works published on and after March 1, 1989*. Specifications for the proper form and placement of the notice are described in this circular.

Works published before January 1, 1978, are governed by the previous copyright law. Under that law, if a work was published under the copyright owner's authority without a proper notice of copyright, all copyright protection for that work was permanently lost in the United States.

The Uruguay Round Agreements Act of 1994 (URAA) (PL 103-465) modified the effect of publication without notice for certain foreign works. Under this Act, copyright is automatically restored, effective January 1, 1996, for certain foreign works placed into the public domain because of lack of proper notice or noncompliance with other legal requirements. Although restoration is automatic, if the copyright owner wishes to enforce rights against reliance parties (those who, relying on the public domain status of a work, were already using the work before the URAA was enacted), he/she must either file with the Copyright Office a Notice of Intent to Enforce the restored copyright or serve such a notice on the reliance party.

For more information about the copyright notice under the law in effect before January 1, 1978, request Circular 96 Section 202.2, "Copyright Notice", from the Copyright Office. For more information about restoration of copyright under the URAA, request Circular 38b, "Highlights of Copyright Amendments Contained in the Uruguay Round Agreements Act (URAA)."

—————————— USE OF THE COPYRIGHT NOTICE ——————————

Copyright is a form of protection provided by the laws of the United States to authors of "original works of authorship." When a work is published under the authority of the copyright owner (see definition of "publication" below), a notice of copyright may be placed on all publicly distributed copies or phonorecords. The use of the notice is the responsibility of the copyright owner and does not require permission from, or registration with, the Copyright Office.

Use of the notice may be important because it informs the public that the work is protected by copyright, identifies the copyright owner, and shows the year of first publication. Furthermore, in the event that a work is infringed, if the work carries a proper notice, the court will not *give any weight to a defendant's interposition of an innocent infringement defense*—that is, that he or she did not realize that the work was protected. An innocent infringement defense may result in a reduction in damages that the copyright owner would otherwise receive.

For works first published on and after March 1, 1989, use of the copyright notice is optional. Before March 1, 1989, the use of the notice was mandatory on all published works. Omitting the notice on any work first published before that date could result in the loss of copyright protection if corrective steps are not taken within a certain amount of time. The curative steps are described in this circular under "Omission of Notice and Errors in Notice."

The Copyright Office does not take a position on whether reprints of works first published with notice before March 1, 1989, which are distributed on or after March 1, 1989, must bear the copyright notice.

WHAT IS PUBLICATION?

The 1976 Copyright Act defines publication as "the distribution of copies or phonorecords of a work to the public by sale or other transfer of ownership, or by rental, lease, or lending." An offering to distribute copies or phonorecords to a group of persons for purposes of further distribution, public performance, or public display also constitutes publication. The following do not constitute publication: printing or other reproduction of copies, performing or displaying a work publicly, or sending copies to the Copyright Office.

COPYRIGHT NOTICE NOT REQUIRED ON UNPUBLISHED WORKS

The copyright notice has never been required on unpublished works. However, because the dividing line between a preliminary distribution and actual publication is sometimes difficult to determine, the copyright owner may wish to place a copyright notice on copies or phonorecords that leave his or her control to indicate that rights are claimed.

An appropriate notice for an unpublished work might be: Unpublished work (C in a circle symbol) 1998 John Doe.

——————————————————— FORM OF NOTICE ———————————————

The form of the copyright notice used for "visually perceptible" copies—that is, those that can be seen or read, either directly (such as books) or with the aid of a machine (such as films)—is different from the form used for phonorecords of sound recordings (such as compact disks or cassettes).

VISUALLY PERCEPTIBLE COPIES

The notice for visually perceptible copies should contain three elements. They should appear together or in close proximity on the copies. The elements are:

1. *The symbol* (the letter C in a circle), or the word "Copyright", or the abbreviation "Copr."; and

2. *The year of first publication.* If the work is a derivative work or a compilation incorporating previously published material, the year date of first publication of the derivative work or compilation is sufficient. Examples of derivative works are translations or dramatizations; an example of a compilation is an anthology. The year may be omitted when a pictorial, graphic, or sculptural work, with accompanying textual matter, if any, is reproduced in or on greeting cards, postcards, stationery, jewelry, dolls, toys, or useful articles; and

3. *The name of the owner of copyright in the work*, or an abbreviation by which the name can be recognized, or a generally known alternative designation of the owner.

Example: (C in a circle symbol) 1999 Jane Doe

The "C in a circle" notice is used only on "visually perceptible" copies. Certain kinds of works, for example, musical, dramatic, and literary works, may be fixed not in "copies" but by means of sound in an audio recording. Since audio recordings such as audio tapes and phonograph disks are "phonorecords" and not "copies", the "C in a circle" notice is not used to indicate protection of the underlying musical, dramatic, or literary work that is recorded.

*The United States is a member of the Universal Copyright Convention (the UCC), which came into force on September 16, 1955. To guarantee protection for a copyrighted work in all UCC member countries, the notice must consist of the symbol (C in a circle symbol)(the word "Copyright" or the abbreviation are not acceptable), the year of first publication, and the name of the copyright proprietor. Example: (C in a circle symbol) 1999 John Doe. For information about international copyright relationships, request Circular 38a, "International Copyright Relations of the United States."

PHONORECORDS OF SOUND RECORDINGS

The copyright notice for phonorecords embodying a sound recording is different from that for other works. Sound recordings are defined as "works that result from the fixation of a series of musical, spoken or other sounds, but not including the sounds accompanying a motion picture or other audiovisual work." Copyright in a sound recording protects the particular series of sounds fixed in the recording against unauthorized reproduction, revision, and distribution. This copyright is distinct from copyright of the musical, literary, or dramatic work that may be recorded on the phonorecord.

Phonorecords may be records (such as LPs and 45s), audio tapes, cassettes, or disks. The notice should contain the following three elements appearing together on the phonorecord:

1. *The symbol* (the letter P in a circle); and

2. *The year of first publication* of the sound recording; and

3. *The name of the owner of copyright* in the sound recording, or an abbreviation by which the name can be recognized, or a generally known alternative designation of the owner. If the producer of the sound recording is named on the phonorecord label or container and if no other name appears in conjunction with the notice, the producer's name shall be considered a part of the notice. Example: (P in a circle symbol) 1999 X.Y.Z. Records, Inc.

————————————————— CONTRIBUTIONS TO COLLECTIVE WORKS

A "collective work" is one in which a number of contributions that are separate and independent works in themselves are assembled into a collective whole. Examples of collective works include periodicals (such as magazines and journals), encyclopedias, and anthologies.

A single copyright notice applicable to the collective work as a whole serves to indicate protection for all the contributions in the collective work, except for advertisements, regardless of the ownership of copyright in the individual contributions and whether they have been published previously.

However, a separate contribution to a collective work may bear its own notice of copyright, and in some cases, it may be advantageous to utilize the separate notice. As a practical matter, a separate notice will inform the public of the identity of the owner of the contribution. For works first published before March 1, 1989, there may be additional reasons to use a separate notice. If the owner of the collective work is not the same as the owner of an individual contribution that does not bear its own notice, the contribution is considered to bear an erroneous notice. (For the effects of a notice with the wrong name, see "Error in Name" on page 5 of this circular.) Additionally, if an individual author of contributions to a periodical wishes to make a single registration for a group of contributions published within a 12-month period, each contribution must carry its own notice. For information on this type of registration, request Form GR/CP and Information Package 104.

A notice for the collective work will not serve as the notice for advertisements inserted on behalf of persons other than the copyright owner of the collective work. These advertisements should each bear a separate notice in the name of the copyright owner of the advertisement.

— PUBLICATIONS INCORPORATING U.S. GOVERNMENT WORKS

Works by the U.S. Government are not eligible for copyright protection. For works published on and after March 1, 1989, the previous notice requirement for works consisting primarily of one or more U.S. Government works has been eliminated. However, use of a notice on such a work will defeat a claim of innocent infringement as previously described *provided* the notice also includes a statement that identifies either those portions of the work in which copyright is claimed or those portions that constitute U.S. Government material. An example is: "(C in a circle symbol) 1998 Ann Doe. Copyright claimed in Chapters 7-10, exclusive of U.S. Government maps."

Copies of works published before March 1, 1989, that consist primarily of one or more works of the U.S. Government should have a notice and the identifying statement.

——————————————————————————— POSITION OF NOTICE

The copyright notice should be placed on copies or phonorecords in such a way that it gives reasonable notice of the claim of copyright. The notice should be permanently legible to an ordinary user of the work under normal conditions of use and should not be concealed from view upon reasonable examination. The Copyright Office has issued regulations, summarized below, concerning the position of the notice and methods of affixation (37 C.F.R., Part 201). To read the complete regulations, request Circular 96 Section 201.20, "Methods of Affixation and Positions of the Copyright Notice on Various Types of Works," or consult the Code of Federal Regulations in your local library.

The following locations and methods of affixation are examples of appropriate position of notice. These examples are not exhaustive.

Works Published in Book Form
  + Title page
  + Page immediately following the title page
  + Either side of the front or back cover
  + First or last page of the main body of the work *Single-leaf Works*

+ Front or back
Works Published as Periodicals or Other Serials
 + Any location acceptable for books
 + As part of, or adjacent to, the masthead or on the page containing
   the masthead
 + Adjacent to a prominent heading, appearing at or near the front of
   the issue, containing the title of the periodical and any
   combination of the volume and issue number and date of the issue
Works Published as Separate Contributions to Collective Works

For a separate contribution reproduced on only one page:
 + Under the title or elsewhere on the same page For a separate
   contribution reproduced on more than one page:
 + Under a title appearing at or near the beginning of the contribution
 + On the first page of the main body of the contribution
 + Immediately following the end of the contribution
 + On any of the pages where the contribution appears if the
   contribution consists of no more than 20 pages, the notice is
   reproduced prominently, and the application of the notice to the
   particular contribution is clear
Works Reproduced in Machine-Readable Copies
 + With or near the title or at the end of the work, on visually
   perceptible printouts
 + At the user's terminal at sign-on
 + On continuous display on the terminal l Reproduced durably on a
   gummed or other label securely affixed to the copies or to a
   container used as a permanent receptacle for the copies
Motion Pictures and Other Audiovisual Works

A notice embodied in the copies by a photomechanical or electronic
process so that it ordinarily would appear whenever the work is
performed in its entirety may be located:
 + With or near the title
 + With the cast, credits, and similar information
 + At or immediately following the beginning of the work
 + At or immediately preceding the end of the work The notice on works
   lasting 60 seconds or less, such as untitled motion pictures or
   other audiovisual works, may be located:
 + In all the locations specified above for longer motion pictures; and
 + If the notice is embodied electronically or photo-mechanically, on
   the leader of the film or tape immediately preceding the work. For
   audiovisual works or motion pictures distributed to the public for

private use, the locations include the above, and in addition:
  + On the permanent housing or container
Pictorial, Graphic, and Sculptural Works

For works embodied in two-dimensional copies, a notice may be affixed
directly, durably, and permanently to:
  + The front or back of the copies;
  + Any backing, mounting, framing, or other material to which the
    copies are durably attached, so as to withstand normal use. For
    works reproduced in three-dimensional copies, a notice may be
    affixed directly, durably, and permanently to:
  + Any visible portion of the work;
  + Any base, mounting, or framing or other material on which the copies
    are durably attached.
For works on which it is impractical to affix a notice to the copies directly or
by means of a durable label, a notice is acceptable if it appears on a tag or
durable label attached to the copy so that it will remain with it as it passes
through commerce.

For works reproduced in copies consisting of sheet-like or strip
material bearing multiple or continuous reproductions of the work, such
as fabrics or wallpaper, the notice may be applied:
  + To the reproduction itself;
  + To the margin, selvage, or reverse side of the material at frequent
    and regular intervals; or
  + If the material contains neither a selvage nor reverse side, to tags
    or labels attached to the copies and to any spools, reels, or
    containers housing them in such a way that the notice is visible in
    commerce.
————— OMISSION OF NOTICE AND ERRORS IN NOTICE —————

The 1976 Copyright Act attempted to ameliorate the strict consequences of
failure to include notice under prior law. It contained provisions that set out
specific corrective steps to cure omissions or errors in notice. Under these
provisions, an applicant had 5 years after publication to cure omission of notice
or certain errors. Although these provisions are technically still in the law, their
impact has been limited by the Berne amendment making notice optional for
all works published on and after March 1, 1989. There may still be instances,
such as the defense of innocent infringement, where the question of proper
notice may be a factor in assessing damages in infringement actions.

Omission Of Notice

"Omission of notice" is publishing without a notice. In addition, some errors are considered the same as omission of notice. These are:
+ A notice that does not contain the (the letter C in a circle symbol), or the word "Copyright" or the abbreviation "Copr." or, if the work is a sound recording, the symbol P (the letter P in a circle);
+ A notice dated more than 1 year later than the date of first publication;
+ A notice without a name or date that could reasonably be considered part of the notice;
+ A notice that lacks the statement required for works consisting preponderantly of U.S. Government material; and
+ A notice located so that it does not give reasonable notice of the claim of copyright.

The omission of notice does not affect the copyright protection, and no corrective steps are required if the work was published on or after March 1, 1989. For works published between January 1, 1978, but before March 1, 1989, no corrective steps are required if:

1. The notice is omitted from no more than a relatively small number of copies or phonorecords distributed to the public; or
2. The omission violated an express written requirement that the published copies or phonorecords bear the prescribed notice.

In all other cases of omission in works published before March 1, 1989, to preserve copyright:

1. The work must have been registered before it was published in any form or before the omission occurred, or it must have been registered within 5 years after the date of publication without notice; and

2. The copyright owner must have made a reasonable effort to add the notice to all copies or phonorecords that were distributed to the public in the United States after the omission was discovered. If these corrective steps were not taken, the work went into the public domain in the United States 5 years after publication. At that time all U.S. copyright protection was lost and cannot be restored.

Error in Year

If the copyright duration depends on the date of first publication and the year given in the notice is earlier than the actual publication date, protection may be shortened by beginning the term on the date in the notice. (For later date in the notice, see "Omission of Notice.")

Example: A work made for hire is created in 1983 and is first published in 1988. However, the notice contains the earlier year of 1987. In this case, the term of copyright protection would be measured from the year in the notice, and the expiration date would be 2082, 95 years from 1987.

Error in Name

When the person named in the notice is not the owner of copyright, the error may be corrected by:

1. Registering the work in the name of the true owner;

or

2. Recording a document in the Copyright Office executed by the person named in the notice that shows the correct ownership. Otherwise, anyone who innocently infringes the copyright and can prove that he or she was misled by the notice and obtained a transfer or license from the person named in the notice may have a complete defense against the infringement.

———————————————————————————————— MANDATORY DEPOSIT

All works under copyright protection and published in the United States on or after March 1, 1989, are subject to mandatory deposit whether published with or without a notice.

Works first published *before* March 1, 1989, are subject to mandatory deposit if they were published in the United States with notice of copyright. In general, within 3 months of publication in the United States, the owner of copyright or of the exclusive right of publication must deposit two copies (or, in the case of sound recordings, two phonorecords) of the work in the Copyright Office for the use or disposition of the Library of Congress.

The Copyright Office has issued regulations exempting certain categories of works entirely from the mandatory de-posit requirements and reducing the obligation for other categories. If copyright registration is sought, the same deposit may be used for the mandatory deposit and for registration. For further information about mandatory deposit, request Circular 7d, "Mandatory Deposit of Copies or Phonorecords for the Library of Congress."

Information via the Internet: Frequently requested circulars, announcements, regulations, other related materials, and all copyright application forms are available via the Internet. You may access these via the Copyright Office homepage at [http://www.loc.gov/copyright].

Information by Fax: Circulars and other information (but not application forms) are available from Fax-on-Demand at (202) 707-2600.

Information by telephone: For information about copyright, call the Public Information Office at (202) 707-3000. The TTY number is (202) 707-6737. Information specialists are on duty in the Public Information Office from 8:30 a.m. to 5:00 p.m. eastern time, Monday through Friday, except federal holidays. Recorded information is available 24 hours a day. Or, if you know which application forms and circulars you want, request them from the Forms and Publications Hotline at (202) 707-9100 24 hours a day. Leave a recorded message.

Information by regular mail:
Write to:
Library of Congress
Copyright Office
Public Information Office
101 Independence Avenue,
S.E. Washington, D.C. 20559-6000

REV: June 1999

Format Note: This electronic version has been altered slightly from the original printed text for presentation on the World Wide Web. For a copy of the original circular, consult the pdf version or write to Copyright Office, 101 Independence Avenue S.E., Washington, D.C. 20559-6000.

———————————————————————————————— 04/04/2000

*****

United States Copyright Office

Circular 15

Renewal of Copyright

===

————————————————————————————————————— IMPORTANT:

+ Public Law 102-307, enacted on June 26, 1992, amended the copyright law to make renewal automatic and renewal registration optional for works originally copyrighted between January 1, 1964, and December 31, 1977.

+ While this amendment to the current law makes renewal registration optional for works copyrighted between January 1, 1964, and December 31, 1977, there are a number of incentives that encourage the filing of a renewal application, especially during the 28th year of the copyright term.

+ Public Law 105-298, enacted on October 27, 1998, amended the copyright law to add 20 years to the copyright term. ———————————————————————

————————————————— THE RENEWAL SYSTEM ————————————————

Under the 1909 copyright law, works copyrighted in the United States before January 1, 1978, were subject to a renewal system in which the term of copyright was divided into two consecutive terms. Renewal registration, within strict time limits, was required as a condition of securing the second term and extending the copyright to its maximum length.

On January 1, 1978, the current copyright law (title 17 of the United States Code) came into effect in the United States. This law retained the renewal system for works that were copyrighted before 1978 and were still in their first terms on January 1, 1978. For these works the statute provides for a first term of copyright protection lasting for 28 years, with the possibility for a second term of 47 years. The 1992 amending legislation automatically secures this second term for works copyrighted between January 1, 1964, and December 31, 1977.

+ If a copyright originally secured before January 1, 1964, was not renewed at the proper time, copyright protection expired at the end of the 28th calendar year of the copyright and could not be restored.

+ WORKS COPYRIGHTED BETWEEN JANUARY 1, 1964, AND
DECEMBER 31, 1977, are affected by P.L. 102-307, which automatically
secured the second term and made renewal registration optional, and by Public
Law 105-298, which added an additional 20 years to the second term of
copyright for these works. The term of copyright in works copyrighted
between January 1, 1964, and December 31, 1977, is now 95 years. There is no
requirement to register a renewal in order to extend the original 28- year
copyright term to the full term of 95 years. Although the renewal term is
secured automatically, the Copyright Office does not issue a renewal certificate
for these works unless a renewal application and fee are received and registered
in the Copyright Office.

The benefits to making a renewal registration during the 28th year of the
original term of copyright are:

1. The renewal copyright vests in the name of the renewal claimant on the
effective date of the renewal registration.

For example, if a renewal registration is made in the 28th year and the renewal
claimant dies following the renewal registration but before the end of the year,
the renewal copyright is secured on behalf of that renewal claimant and the 67
years of renewal copyright become a part of that individual's estate.

NOTE: If the renewal registration is not made in the 28th year, the renewal
copyright will vest on the first day of the renewal term in the party entitled to
claim renewal as of December 31 of the 28th year.

2. The Copyright Office issues a renewal certificate, which constitutes prima
facie evidence as to the validity of the copyright during the renewed and
extended term and of the facts stated in the certificate.

3. The right to use the derivative work in the extended term may be affected.

For example, if an author dies before the 28th year of the original term and a
statutory renewal claimant registers a renewal within the 28th year, that
claimant can terminate an assignment made by the deceased author authorizing
the exploitation of a derivative work. If a renewal is not made during the 28th
year, a derivative work created during the first term of copyright under a prior
grant can continue to be used according to the terms of the grant. Thus, an

author or other renewal claimant loses the right to object to the continued use of the derivative work during the second term by failing to make a timely renewal, but any terms in the prior grant concerning payment or use, e.g., a royalty, must continue to be honored. This exception does not apply to a new derivative work, which can only be prepared with the consent of the author or other renewal claimant.

A renewal registration made after the 28th year will not confer the benefits mentioned above but will confer other benefits denied to unregistered works. For example, renewal registration establishes a public record of copyright ownership in a work at the time that the renewal was registered. The courts have discretion to determine the evidentiary weight accorded a certificate of renewal registration when registration is made after the 28th year of the copyright term. Renewal registration is a prerequisite to statutory damages and attorney's fees for published works not registered for the original term.

In cases where no original registration or renewal registration is made before the expiration of the 28th year, important benefits can still be secured by filing a renewal registration at any time during the renewal term. These benefits would include, for example, statutory damages and attorney's fees in any infringement suit for infringements occurring after the renewal registration is made. Also, it is a requirement to get into court in certain circumstances under section 411 (a), and it creates a public record both to defend against innocent infringers and to facilitate easier licensing of the work.

———————————————— RENEWAL FILING PERIOD ————————————————

For works copyrighted between January 1, 1964, and December 31,1977, an application for renewal of copyright can be made:

+ within the last (28th) calendar year of the original term of copyright or + at any time during the renewed and extended term of 67 years.

To determine the filing period for renewal during the original term:

1. First, determine the date of original copyright for the work. (In the case of works originally registered in unpublished form, copyright began on the date of registration; for published works, copyright began on the date of first publication with copyright notice.)

2. Then add 28 years to the year the work was originally copyrighted.

This will determine the calendar year during which the copyright becomes eligible for renewal with a renewal filing during the original term due by December 31 of that year. An exception to this rule exists when the copyright notice in the work contains a year date earlier than the year date of first publication. In this case, the renewal filing period is computed from the year date in the copyright notice. For example, a work published January 20, 1975, contains a copyright notice reading "Copyright 1974 by Anderson Homes." Compute the 28-year original term from the year 1974.

To renew a copyright during the original copyright term, the renewal application and fee must be received in the Copyright Office during the 28th year of the original term of copyright. All terms of original copyright run through the end of the 28th calendar year making the period for renewal registration in the original term from December 31 of the 27th year of the copyright through December 31 of the following year.

Note: The Copyright Office does not notify authors or claimants when the copyrights in their works become eligible for renewal.

============= WHO MAY CLAIM RENEWAL =============

Renewal copyright may be claimed only by those persons specified in the law.

A. The following persons may claim renewal in all types of works except those enumerated in Paragraph B below:

1. The author, if living, may claim as the author.

2. If the author is dead, the widow or widower of the author, or the child or children of the author, or both, may claim as the widow of the author or the widower of the author and/or the child of the deceased author or the children of the deceased author.

3. If there is no surviving widow, widower, or child, and the author left a will, the author's executors may claim as the executors of the author.

4. If there is no surviving widow, widower, or child, and the author left no will or the will has been discharged, the next of kin may claim as the next of kin of the deceased author, there being no will.

B. Only in the case of the following four types of works may the copyright proprietor (owner) claim renewal:

1. Posthumous work (a work published after the author's death as to which no copyright assignment or other contract for exploitation has occurred during the deceased author's lifetime). Renewal may be claimed as proprietor of copyright in a posthumous work.

2. Periodical, cyclopedic, or other composite work. Renewal may be claimed as proprietor of copyright in a composite work.

3. Work copyrighted by a corporate body otherwise than as assignee or licensee of the individual author. Renewal may be claimed as proprietor of copyright in a work copyrighted by a corporate body otherwise than as assignee or licensee of the individual author. (This type of claim is considered appropriate in relatively few cases.)

4. Work copyrighted by an employer for whom such work was made for hire. Renewal may be claimed as proprietor of copyright in a work made for hire.

For registration in the 28th year of the original copyright term, the renewal claimant is the individual(s) or entity who is entitled to claim renewal copyright on the date the application is filed.

For registration after the 28th year of the original copyright term, the renewal claimant is the individual(s) or entity who is entitled to claim renewal copyright on December 31 of the 28th year.

========= HOW TO REGISTER A RENEWAL CLAIM ==========

APPLICATION FORM

Application for renewal registration must be filed on Form RE, which is supplied by the Copyright Office on request. It is also available from the Copyright Office Website at http://www.loc.gov/copyright.

RENEWAL FEE

The filing fee for a renewal application is $45*. If several applications are submitted at the same time, a remittance for the total amount should accompany them.

———————— *NOTE: Fees are effective through June 30, 2002. After that date, check the Copyright Office Website at http://www.loc.gov/copyright or call (202) 707-3000 for current fee information. ————————————

All remittances should be in the form of drafts (that is, checks, money orders, or bank drafts) payable to: Register of Copyrights. Do not send cash. The Copyright Office cannot assume any responsibility for the loss of currency sent in payment of copyright fees.

Drafts must be redeemable without service or exchange fee through a U.S. institution, must be payable in U.S. dollars, and must be imprinted with American Banking Association routing numbers.

If a check received in payment of the filing fee is returned to the Copyright Office as uncollectible, the Copyright Office will cancel the registration and will notify the applicant. The fee for processing a renewal claim is nonrefundable, whether or not renewal registration is ultimately made.

ORIGINAL AND RENEWAL REGISTRATION DURING THE 28TH YEAR

An original registration can be made only during the first 28-year term of copyright protection. However, it is possible to make both an original registration and a renewal registration during the 28th year of the copyright term. This requires filing the appropriate basic application form, accompanied by deposit copies and a $30* filing fee, and a Form RE and a $45* filing fee.

RENEWAL REGISTRATION WITHOUT ORIGINAL REGISTRATION

A renewal registration may be made without making an original registration during the 28th year of the original term. A renewal application Form RE must be filed, accompanied by the Form RE Addendum, a copy of the work as first published or appropriate identifying material in accordance with the requirements of 37 CFR 202.20 and 202.21, and the filing fee. (Request Circular 96 202.17 for further information.)

The information in the Form RE Addendum is necessary to establish that copyright subsists in the original term which is capable of renewal. The deposit copy facilitates the examination of the claim to copyright which is submitted for renewal, and it is available for accession by the Library of Congress to its collections for the benefit of the nation.

A single $60* fee will be required for a renewal registration using Form RE and Form RE Addendum. Please contact the Renewals Section in the Copyright Office for more information. Phone the Renewals Section at (202) 707-8180 or fax at (202) 707-3849 or write to the Copyright Office at:

Library of Congress
Copyright Office
Renewals Section, LM-449
101 Independence Avenue, S.E.
Washington, D.C. 20559-6000

================== NEW VERSIONS ==================

Copyright in a new version of a previously copyrighted work (such as an arrangement, translation, dramatization, compilation, or work republished with new matter) covers only the additions, changes, or other new material appearing for the first time in that version. The copyright secured in a new version is independent of any copyright protection in material published or copyrighted earlier, and the only "authors" of a new version are those who contributed copyrightable matter to it. Thus, for renewal purposes, the person who wrote the original version upon which the new work is based cannot be regarded as an "author" of the new version, unless that person also contributed to the new matter.

===================== CONTRIBUTIONS TO PERIODICALS OR OTHER COMPOSITE WORKS =========================

SEPARATE RENEWAL FOR A SINGLE CONTRIBUTION

Separate renewal registration is possible for a work published as a contribution to a periodical, serial, or other composite work whether or not the contribution was copyrighted independently or as part of the larger work in which it appeared. Except in the cases described in the next paragraph, each contribution published in a separate issue requires a separate renewal registration.

RENEWAL FOR A GROUP OF CONTRIBUTIONS

+ Requirements for Group Renewal: A renewal registration using a single application and $45*, plus $15* for each addendum, (if required) fee can be made for a group of periodical contributions if all the following five statutory conditions are met:

1. All the works were written by the same author, who is or was an individual (not an employee for hire);

2. All of the works were first published as contributions to periodicals (including newspapers) and were copyrighted on their first publication;

3. The renewal claimant or claimants and the basis of the claim or claims are the same for all the works;

4. The renewal application and fee are received not less than 27 years after the 31st day of December of the calendar year in which all the works were first published; and

5. The renewal application identifies each work separately, including the periodical containing it and the date of first publication.

+ TIME LIMITS FOR GROUP RENEWALS: To be renewed as a group, all the contributions must have been first published during the same calendar year. For example, suppose six contributions by the same author were published on April 1, 1971; July 1, 1971; November 1, 1971; February 1, 1972; July 1, 1972; and March 1, 1973. The three 1971 copyrights can be combined and renewed on the same Form RE at any time during 1999; the two 1972 copyrights can be renewed as a group during 2000; but the 1973 copyright must be renewed by itself in 2001.

======== NOTICE OF RENEWAL OF COPYRIGHT ==========

The Copyright Office is frequently asked whether the notice of copyright should be changed on copies of a work issued during the renewal term. The copyright law is silent on this point, and the continued use of the original form of notice may therefore be considered appropriate. However, a notice that also refers to the fact of renewal might be regarded as more informative and, hence, preferable; for example:

> Copyright 1972 Bobby Eroica Dupea
> Copyright Renewed 1999 by Rayette Depesto

========= EFFECTIVE DATE OF REGISTRATION =========

A renewal registration is effective on the date the Copyright Office receives all the required renewal elements in acceptable form, regardless of how long it then takes to process the application and mail the certificate of registration. The time the Copyright Office requires to process an application varies, depending on the amount of material the Office is receiving. Please keep in mind that it may take a number of days for mailed material to reach the Copyright Office and for the certificate of registration to reach the recipient after being mailed by the Copyright Office.

If you file an application for renewal registration in the Copyright Office, you will not receive an acknowledgment that your application has been received, but you can expect:

+ A letter or telephone call from a copyright examiner or other staff
  member if further information is needed;
+ A certificate of registration to indicate the renewal has been
  registered;
+ If renewal registration cannot be made, a letter explaining why it has
  been refused.
If you want to know when the Copyright Office receives your material, send it by registered or certified mail and request a return receipt from the U.S. Postal Service. Allow at least 4-6 weeks for the return of your receipt.

If you need additional application forms for renewal registration, call (202) 707-9100 anytime, day or night, to record your request on the Copyright Office Forms and Publications Hotline. Please specify the number of forms you need.

You may photocopy blank application forms; however, photocopied forms submitted to the Copyright Office must be clear and legible on a good grade of 8-1/2 inch by 11 inch white paper suitable for automatic feeding through a photocopier. The forms should be printed, preferably in black ink, head-to-head (so that when you turn the sheet over, the top of page 2 is directly behind the top of page 1). FORMS NOT MEETING THESE REQUIREMENTS WILL BE RETURNED TO THE ORIGINATOR.

If, after reading this circular, you have additional questions about
renewal of copyright, you may call the Renewals Section of the Examining
Division at (202) 707-8180 or fax at (202) 707-3849 or write to the
Copyright Office at this address:
Library of Congress
Copyright Office
Renewals Section, LM-449
101 Independence Avenue, S.E.
Washington, D.C. 20559-6000

=========== FOR FURTHER INFORMATION =============

INFORMATION VIA THE INTERNET: Frequently requested circulars, announcements, regulations, other related materials, and all copyright application forms are available via the Internet. You may access these via the Copyright Office homepage at http://www.loc.gov/copyright.

INFORMATION BY FAX: Circulars and other information (but not application forms) are available by Fax-on-Demand at (202)707-2600.

INFORMATION BY TELEPHONE: For general information about copyright, call the Copyright Public Information Office at (202)707-3000. The TTY number is (202)707-6737. Information specialists are on duty from 8:30 a.m. to 5:00 p.m., eastern time, Monday through Friday, except federal holidays. Recorded information is available 24 hours a day. Or, if you know which application forms and circulars you want, request them from the Forms and Publications Hotline at (202)707-9100 24 hours a day. Leave a recorded message.

Information by regular mail:
Write to:
Library of Congress
Copyright Office
Publications Section, LM-455
101 Independence Avenue, S.E.
Washington, D.C. 20559-6000
———————————————————— Library of Congress Copyright Office 101 Independence Avenue, S.E. Washington, D.C. 20559-6000

http://www.loc.gov/copyright
REV: June 1999 — 15,000
WEB REV: June 1999
U.S. GOVERNMENT PRINTING OFFICE: 1999-454-879/4
*****

United States Copyright Office

Circular 15t

Extension of Copyright Terms

===

23

============= PURPOSE OF THIS CIRCULAR =============

This circular will inform you of the provisions in the copyright statute affecting the duration of subsisting copyrights and give you some information with examples illustrating what these provisions mean. For works copyrighted for the first time on or after January 1, 1978, the statutory provisions governing the duration of protection are quite different and are not included in this circular. For general information about duration of copyright under the current law, request Circular 15a, "Duration of Copyright."

===
EFFECT OF 1976 COPYRIGHT LAW WITH AMENDMENTS OF 1992 AND   1998
===

The Copyright Act of October 1976 (Public Law 94-553, 90 Stat. 2541, amending title 17 of the United States Code), effective January 1, 1978, has been amended to extend the term of copyright on two subsequent occasions with the passage of the Copyright Amendments Act of 1992 (Public Law 102-307, 10 6 Stat. 266, amending section 304 of title 17 of the United States Code), and the Sonny Bono Copyright Term Extension Act of 1998 (Public Law 105-298, 112 Stat. 2827, amending chapter 3 of title 17 of the United States Code).

Public Law 102-307, enacted on June 26, 1992, amended the copyright law to make renewal automatic and renewal registration optional for works originally copyrighted between January 1, 1964, and December 31, 1977.

Public Law 105-298, enacted on October 27, 1998, added an additional 20 years to the overall term of copyright protection.

—2—

+ COPYRIGHTS ALREADY IN THEIR SECOND TERM ON JANYARY 1, 1978: The duration of the copyright term has automatically been prolonged to last for a total of 95 years. No further renewal registration is necessary.

+ COPYRIGHTS IN THEIR FIRST TERM ON JANUARY 1, 1978: Renewal registration was still necessary to obtain the second term for works copyrighted between January 1, 1950, and December 31, 1963. Renewal registration is optional for works copyrighted between January 1, 1964, and December 31, 1977. In both cases, the renewal copyright is longer than the term in effect before 1978. The renewal term extends the copyright for a full term of 95 years.

===
COPYRIGHTS IN THEIR SECOND TERM: AUTOMATIC EXTENSION OF DURATION
===

RENEWED COPYRIGHTS AUTOMATICALLY EXTENDED TO MAXIMUM OF 95 YEARS

Under the statute, copyrights that had already been renewed and were in their second term at any time between December 31, 1976, and December 31, 1977, inclusive, were automatically extended in duration. The total length of these copyrights is now 95 years from the end of the year in which they were originally secured.

EXAMPLE: A work that was first copyrighted on April 10, 1923, and renewed between April 10, 1950, and April 10, 1951, would formerly have fallen into the public domain after April 10, 1979. The current law extends this copyright through the end of 2018.

These second-term copyrights cannot be renewed again. Under the law, their extension to the maximum 95-year term is automatic and requires no action in the Copyright Office.

A SPECIAL SITUATION: COPYRIGHTS REGISTERED FOR RENEWAL BETWEEN DECEMBER 31, 1976, AND DECEMBER 31, 1977

The automatic extension also applied to copyrights that were the subject of a renewal registration between December 31, 1976, and December 31, 1977, even though their second term was not scheduled to commence until sometime in 1978.

EXAMPLE: A work was first copyrighted on July 29, 1950, and a renewal registration was made on September 1, 1977. The second term of copyright was automatically extended through the end of 2045 without the need of any further renewal.

ANOTHER SPECIAL SITUATION: COPYRIGHTS MORE THAN 56 YEARS OLD

The automatic extension applies not only to copyrights less than 56 years old but also to older copyrights that have previously been extended in duration under a series of Congressional enactments beginning in 1962. [1] As in the case of all other copyrights subsisting in their second term between December 31, 1976, and December 31, 1977, inclusive, these copyrights will expire at the end of the calendar year in which the 95th anniversary of the original date of copyright occurs, so long as the copyright was still in its renewal phase at the time Public Law 105-298 became effective. [2]

EXAMPLE: A work that was first entered for copyright on October 5, 1907, and renewed in 1935, would formerly have fallen into the public domain after October 5, 1963. The first Act extended the copyright to December 31, 1965; the second Act extended it to December 31, 1967; the third Act extended it to December 31, 1968; the fourth Act extended it to December 31, 1969; the fifth Act extended it to December 31, 1970; the sixth Act extended it to December 31, 1971; the seventh Act extended it to December 31, 1972; the eighth Act extended it to December 31, 1974; the ninth Act extended it to December 31, 1976, and the Copyright Act of 1976 finally extended the copyright through the end of 1982 (75 years from the end of the year in which the copyright was originally secured).

===
COPYRIGHTS SECURED BETWEEN JANUARY 1, 1950, AND DECEMBER 31, 1963: RENEWAL WAS NECESSARY
===

Copyrights whose first 28-year term of copyright was secured between January 1, 1950, and December 31, 1963, including works protected in their first term under the Universal Copyright Convention, still had to be renewed within strict time limits in order to receive the maximum statutory duration. U.S. adherence to the Berne Convention did not alter this requirement. Renewal registration had to be made within a year period beginning on December 31 of the

—3—

27th year of the copyright and running through December 31 of the following year.

If a valid renewal registration was made at the proper time, the second term lasts for 67 years. This is 39 years longer than the 28-year renewal term provided under the 1909 law and makes the two terms of protection for the renewed copyright last for a total of 95 years. However, if renewal registration was not made within the statutory time limits, these copyrights expired at the end of their first terms and protection was lost permanently.

===
COPYRIGHTS SECURED BETWEEN JANUARY 1, 1964, AND DECEMBER 31, 1977
===

The amendment to the copyright law enacted June 26, 1992, makes renewal registration optional, and the amendment enacted October 27, 1998, further extends the renewal term to 67 years. The copyright is still divided between a 28-year original term and a 67-year renewal term, but the renewal term automatically vests on December 31st of the 28th year. A renewal registration is not required to secure the renewal copyright. Certain benefits accrue to making renewal registrations, and the Copyright Office continues to accept renewal applications. See Circular 15, "Renewal of Copyright," for a discussion of the benefits of making renewal registration.

===
OTHER STATUTORY PROVISIONS AFFECTING SUBSISTING COPYRIGHTS
===

YEAR-END EXPIRATION OF COPYRIGHTTERMS

The law provides that all terms of copyright will run through the end of the calendar year in which they would otherwise expire. This affects the duration of all copyrights, including those subsisting in either their first or second term in January 1, 1978. For works eligible for renewal registration, the renewal filing period begins on December 31st of the 27th year of the copyright term and ends on December 31st of the 28th year of the copyright term.

TERMINATION OF GRANTS

For works already under statutory copyright on January 1, 1978, the law also contains special provisions allowing the termination of any grant of rights made by an author and covering any part of the period (usually 39 years) that has now been added to the end of the renewal copyright. This right to reclaim ownership of all or any part of the extended term is optional. It can be exercised only by certain persons (the author, or specified heirs of the author), and it must be exercised in accordance with prescribed conditions and within strict time limits.

======== A CHECKLIST OF POINTS TO REMEMBER ========

+ Copyrights already in their second term on January 1, 1978, have been
  automatically extended up to a maximum of 95 years without the need for
  further renewal.
+ Copyrights secured between January 1, 1950, and December 31, 1963, had
  to be renewed within a strict 1-year time limit; if not renewed they
  expired at the end of their 28th calendar year.
+ Copyrights secured between January 1, 1964, and December 31, 1977, are
  renewed automatically even if renewal registration is not made; renewal
  registration is optional and if timely made, entitles the claimant to a
  presumption of validity and other advantages.
+ Works in the public domain cannot be protected by copyright. The 1976
  Act, the 1992 amendment, and the 1998 amendment do not provide a
  procedure for restoring protection for works in which copyright has
  been lost for any reason.
+ Exception: Under the provisions of the Uruguay Round Agreements Act
  (URAA), certain foreign works whose U.S. copyright protection had been
  lost because of non-compliance with formalities of U.S. law were
  restored as of January 1, 1996. Such works may be registered using Form
  GATT. For more information, request Circular 38b, "Highlights of
  Copyright Amendments Contained in the Uruguay Round Agreements Act
  (URAA-GATT)."
+ A work published before January 1, 1964, and originally copyrighted within
the past 75 years may still be protected by copyright if a valid renewal
registration was made during the 28th year of the first term of the copyright.
If renewed and if still valid under the other provisions of the law, the copyright
will now expire 95 years from the end of the year in which it was first secured.
Works published before January 1, 1923, have fallen into the public domain,
but works published after that date could still be protected by copyright if the
copyright was renewed by registration or automatically by law under Public
Law 102-307.

============= FOR FURTHER INFORMATION ===========

INFORMATION VIA THE INTERNET: Frequently requested circulars,
announcements, regulations, other related materials, and all copyright
application forms are available via the Internet. You may access these via the
Copyright Office homepage at http://www.loc.gov/copyright.

INFORMATION BY FAX: Circulars and other information (but not application forms) are available by Fax-on-Demand at (202)707-2600.

INFORMATION BY TELEPHONE: For general information about copyright, call the Copyright Public Information Office at (202)707-3000. The TTY number is (202)707-6737. Information specialists are on duty from 8:30 a.m. to 5:00 p.m., eastern time, Monday through Friday, except federal holidays. Recorded information is available 24 hours a day. Or, if you know which application forms and circulars you want, request them from the Forms and Publications Hotline at (202)707-9100 24 hours a day. Leave a recorded message.

Information by regular mail: Write to:

Library of Congress
Copyright Office
Publications Section, LM-455
101 Independence Avenue, S.E.
Washington, D.C. 20559-6000
——————— ENDNOTES

1 The enactments were Public Laws 87-668, 89-142, 90-141, 90-416, 91-147, 91-555, 92-170, 92-566, and 93-573. Their effect was to extend the second term of all renewed copyrights scheduled to expire between September 19, 1962, and December 3, 1976, through the end of 1976.

2 Works published before January 1, 1923, would have fallen into the public domain at the end of calendar year 1997. Consequently, these works do not receive the additional 20 years of copyright protection created by Public Law 105-298.

____ U.S. GOVERNMENT PRINTING OFFICE: 1999-454-879/5 Library of Congress Copyright Office 101 Independence Avenue, S.E. Washington, D.C. 20559-6000

www.loc.gov/copyright

June 1999 — 15,000
WEB REV: June 1999
*****

United States Copyright Office

Circular 22

How to Investigate the Copyright Status of a Work

===

IN GENERAL

Methods of Approaching & Copyright Investigation

There are several ways to investigate whether a work is under copyright protection and, if so, the facts of the copyright. These are the main ones:

1. Examine a copy of the work for such elements as a copyright notice, place and date of publication, author and publisher. If the work is a sound recording, examine the disk, tape cartridge, or cassette in which the recorded sound is fixed, or the album cover, sleeve, or container in which the recording is sold.

2. Make a search of the Copyright Office catalogs and other records; or

3. Have the Copyright Office make a search for you.

A Few Words of Caution About Copyright Investigations

Copyright investigations often involve more than one of these methods. Even if you follow all three approaches, the results may not be conclusive. Moreover, as explained in this circular, the changes brought about under the Copyright Act of 1976, the Berne Convention Implementation Act of 1988, the Copyright Renewal Act of 1992, and the Sonny Bono Copyright Term Extension Act of 1998 must be considered when investigating the copyright status of a work.

This circular offers some practical guidance on what to look for if you are making a copyright investigation. It is important to realize, however, that this circular contains only general information and that there are a number of exceptions to the principles outlined here. In many cases it is important to consult with a copyright attorney before reaching any conclusions regarding the copyright status of a work.

———————————————————— HOW TO SEARCH COPYRIGHT OFFICE CATALOGS AND RECORDS ————————————————————

Catalog of Copyright Entries

The Copyright Office published the Catalog of Copyright Entries (CCE) in printed format from 1891 through 1978. From 1979 through 1982 the CCE was issued in microfiche format. The catalog was divided into parts according to the classes of works registered. Each CCE segment covered all registrations made during a particular period of time. Renewal registrations made from 1979 through 1982 are found in Section 8 of the catalog. Renewals prior to that time were generally listed at the end of the volume containing the class of work to which they pertained.

A number of libraries throughout the United States maintain copies of the Catalog, and this may provide a good starting point if you wish to make a search yourself. There are some cases, however, in which a search of the Catalog alone will not be sufficient to provide the needed information.
For example:
+ Because the Catalog does not include entries for assignments or other recorded documents, it cannot be used for searches involving the ownership of rights.

+ The Catalog entry contains the essential facts concerning a registration, but it is not a verbatim transcript of the registration record. It does not contain the address of the copyright claimant.

Effective with registrations made since 1982 when the CCE was discontinued, the only method of searching outside the Library of Congress is by using the Internet to access the automated catalog. The automated catalog contains entries from 1978 to the present. Information for accessing the catalog via the Internet is provided below.

Individual Searches of Copyright Records

The Copyright Office is located in the Library of Congress James Madison Memorial Building, 101 Independence Avenue, S.E., Washington, D.C. 20559-6000.

Most Copyright Office records are open to public inspection and searching from 8:30 a.m. to 5 p.m., eastern time, Monday through Friday, except federal holidays.

The various records freely available to the public include an extensive card catalog, an automated catalog containing records from 1978 forward, record books, and microfilm records of assignments and related documents.

Other records, including correspondence files and deposit copies, are not open to the public for searching.

However, they may be inspected upon request and payment of a $65 per hour search fee. [1]

If you wish to do your own searching in the Copyright Office files open to the public, you will be given assistance in locating the records you need and in learning procedures for searching. If the Copyright Office staff actually makes the search for you, a search fee must be charged. The search will not be done while you wait. In addition, the following files dating from 1978 forward are now available over the Internet: COHM, which includes all material except serials and documents; COHD, which includes documents; and COHS, which includes serials.

The Internet site addresses for the Copyright Office files are:
World Wide Web: www.loc.gov/copyright
Telnet: locis.loc.gov
Access to LOCIS requires Telnet support. If your online service provider supports Telnet, you can connect to LOCIS through the World Wide Web or directly by using Telnet.

The Copyright Office does not offer search assistance to users on the Internet.
———————— SEARCHING BY THE COPYRIGHT OFFICE ————

In General

Upon request, the Copyright Office staff will search its records at the statutory rate of $65 [1] for each hour or fraction of an hour consumed. Based on the information you furnish, we will provide an estimate of the total search fee. If you decide to have the Office staff conduct the search, you should send the estimated amount with your request. The Office will then proceed with the search and send you a typewritten report or, if you prefer, an oral report by telephone. If you request an oral report, please provide a telephone number where you can be reached from 8:30 a.m. to 5 p.m., eastern time.

Search reports can be certified on request for an extra fee of $65 per hour. [1] Certified searches are most frequently requested to meet the evidentiary requirements of litigation.

Your request and any other correspondence should be addressed to :

Library of Congress
Copyright Office
Reference and Bibliography Section, LM-451
101 Independence Avenue, S.E.
Washington, D.C. 20559-6000
Tel: (202) 707-6850
Fax: (202) 252-3485
TTY:(202) 707-6737
What the Fee Does Not Cover

The search fee does not include the cost of additional certificates, photocopies of deposits, or copies of other Office records. For information concerning these services, request Circular 6, "Obtaining Access to and Copies of Copyright Office Records and Deposits."

Information Needed

The more detailed information you can furnish with your request, the less expensive the search will be. Please provide as much of the following information as possible:

+ The title of the work, with any possible variants + The names of the authors, including possible pseudonyms + The name of the probable copyright owner, which may be the publisher or producer + The approximate year when the work was published or registered + The type of work involved (book, play, musical composition, sound recording, photograph, etc.) + For a work originally published as a part of a periodical or collection, the title of that publication and any other information, such as the volume or issue number, to help identify it + The registration number or any other copyright data

Motion pictures are often based on other works such as books or serialized contributions to periodicals or other composite works. *If you desire a search for an underlying work or for music from a motion picture, you must specifically request such a search. You must also identify the underlying works and music and furnish the specific titles, authors, and approximate dates of these works.*

Searches Involving Assignments and Other Documents Affecting Copyright Ownership

For the standard hourly search fee, the Copyright Office staff will search its indexes covering the records of assignments and other recorded documents concerning ownership of copyrights. The reports of searches in these cases will state the facts shown in the Office's indexes of the recorded documents but will offer no interpretation of the content of the documents or their legal effect.

———————————— LIMITATIONS ON SEARCHES ————————————

In determining whether or not to have a search made, you should keep the following points in mind:

NO SPECIAL LISTS. The Copyright Office does not maintain any listings of works by subject or any lists of works that are in the public domain.

CONTRIBUTIONS NOT LISTED SEPARATELY IN COPYRIGHT OFFICE RECORDS. Individual works such as stories, poems, articles, or musical compositions that were published as contributions to a copyrighted periodical or collection are usually not listed separately by title in our records.

NO COMPARISONS. The Copyright Office does not search or compare copies of works to determine questions of possible infringement or to determine how much two or more versions of a work have in common.

TITLES AND NAMES NOT COPYRIGHTABLE. Copyright does not protect names and titles, and our records list many different works identified by the same or similar titles. Some brand names, trade names, slogans, and phrases may be entitled to protection under the general rules of law relating to unfair competition. They may also be entitled to registration under the provisions of the trademark laws. Questions about the trademark laws should be addressed to the Commissioner of Patents and Trademarks, Washington, D.C. 20231. Possible protection of names and titles under common law principles of unfair competition is a question of state law.

NO LEGAL ADVICE. The Copyright Office cannot express any opinion as to the legal significance or effect of the facts included in a search report.

SOME WORDS OF CAUTION

Searches Not Always Conclusive

Searches of the Copyright Office catalogs and records are useful in helping to determine the copyright status of a work, but they cannot be regarded as conclusive in all cases. The complete absence of any information about a work in the Office records does not mean that the work is unprotected. The following are examples of cases in which information about a particular work may be incomplete or lacking entirely in the Copyright Office:

+ Before 1978, unpublished works were entitled to protection under
  common law without the need of registration.
+ Works published with notice prior to 1978 may be registered at any
  time within the first 28-year term.
+ Works copyrighted between January 1, 1964, and December 31, 1977, are affected by the Copyright Renewal Act of 1992, which automatically extends the copyright term and makes renewal registrations optional.

+ For works under copyright protection on or after January 1, 1978, registration may be made at any time during the term of protection. Although registration is not required as a condition of copyright protection, there are certain definite advantages to registration. For further information, request Circular 1, "Copyright Basics."

+ Since searches are ordinarily limited to registrations that have already been cataloged, a search report may not cover recent registrations for which catalog records are not yet available.

+ The information in the search request may not have been complete or
  specific enough to identify the work.
+ The work may have been registered under a different title or as part of
  a larger work.
Protection in Foreign Countries

Even if you conclude that a work is in the public domain in the United States, this does not necessarily mean that you are free to use it in other countries. Every nation has its own laws governing the length and scope of copyright protection, and these are applicable to uses of the work within that nation's borders. Thus, the expiration or loss of copyright protection in the United States may still leave the work fully protected against unauthorized use in other countries.

OTHER CIRCULARS

For further information, request Circular 6, "Obtaining Access to and Copies of Copyright Office Records and Deposits"; Circular 15, "Renewal of Copyright"; Circular 15a, "Duration of Copyright"; and Circular 15t, "Extension of Copyright Terms," from:

Library of Congress
Copyright Office
Publications Section, LM-455
101 Independence Avenue, S.E.
Washington, D.C. 20559-6000

You may call the Forms and Publications Hotline (202) 707-9100 at any time, day or night, to leave a recorded request for forms or circulars. Requests are filled and mailed promptly.

——————————————————————— IMPACT OF COPYRIGHT ACT ON COPYRIGHT INVESTIGATIONS ———————————————————————

On October 19, 1976, the President signed into law a complete revision of the copyright law of the United States (title 17 of the United States Code). Most provisions of this statute came into force on January 1, 1978, superseding the copyright act of 1909. These provisions made significant changes in the copyright law. Further important changes resulted from the Berne Convention Implementation Act of 1988, which took effect March 1, 1989; the Copyright Renewal Act of 1992 (P.L. 102-307) enacted June 26, 1992, which amended the renewal provisions of the copyright law; and the Sonny Bono Copyright Term Extension Act of 1998 (P.L. 105-298) enacted October 27, 1998, which extended the term of copyrights for an additional 20 years.

If you need more information about the provisions of either the 1909 or the 1976 law, write or call the Copyright Office. For information about the Berne Convention Implementation Act, request Circular 93, "Highlights of U.S. Adherence to the Berne Convention." For information about renewals, request Circular 15, "Renewal of Copyright." For information about the Sonny Bono Copyright Term Extension Act, request SL-15, "New Terms for Copyright Protection." Copies of the law are now $14.00 each. Request "Copyright Law, Circular 92," (stock number is changed to 030-002-00195-1) from:

Superintendent of Documents
P.O. Box 371954
Pittsburgh, PA 15250-7954
Tel: (202) 512-1800
Fax: (202) 512-2250

For copyright investigations, the following points about the impact of the Copyright Act of 1976, the Berne Convention Implementation Act of 1988, and the Copyright Renewal Act of 1992 should be considered:

A Changed System of Copyright Formalities

Some of the most sweeping changes under the 1976 Copyright Act involve copyright formalities, that is, the procedural requirements for securing and maintaining full copyright protection. The old system of formalities involved copyright notice, deposit and registration, recordation of transfers and licenses of copyright ownership, and United States manufacture, among other things. In general, while retaining formalities, the 1976 law reduced the chances of mistakes, softened the consequences of errors and omissions, and allowed for the correction of errors.

The Berne Convention Implementation Act of 1988 reduced formalities, most notably making the addition of the previously mandatory copyright notice optional. It should be noted that the amended notice requirements are not retroactive.

The Copyright Renewal Act of 1992, enacted June 26, 1992, automatically extends the term of copyrights secured between January 1, 1964, and December 31, 1977, making renewal registration optional. Consult Circular 15, "Renewal of Copyright," for details. For additional information, you may contact the Renewals Section.

Tel: (202) 707-8180
Fax: (202) 707-3849
Automatic Copyright

Under the present copyright law, copyright exists in original works of authorship created and fixed in any tangible medium of expression, now known or later developed, from which they can be perceived, reproduced, or otherwise communicated, either directly, or indirectly with the aid of a machine or device. In other words, copyright is an incident of creative authorship not dependent on statutory formalities. Thus, registration with the Copyright Office generally is not required, but there are certain advantages that arise from a timely registration. For further information on the advantages of registration, write or call the Copyright Office and request Circular 1, "Copyright Basics."

Copyright Notice

The 1909 Copyright Act and the 1976 Copyright Act as originally enacted required a notice of copyright on published works. For most works, a copyright notice consisted of the symbol (C in a circle), the word "Copyright," or the abbreviation "Copr.," together with the name of the owner of copyright and the year of first publication. For example: "(C in a circle symbol) Joan Crane 1994" or "Copyright 1994 by Abraham Adams."

For sound recordings published on or after February 15, 1972, a copyright notice might read "1994 XYZ Records, Inc." See below for more information about sound recordings.

For mask works, a copyright notice might read "(C in a circle symbol) SDR Industries." Request Circular 100, "Federal Statutory Protection for Mask Works," for more information.
As originally enacted, the 1976 law prescribed that all visually perceptible published copies of a work, or published phonorecords of a sound recording, should bear a proper copyright notice. This applies to such works published before March 1, 1989. After March 1, 1989, notice of copyright on these works is optional. Adding the notice, however, is strongly encouraged and, if litigation involving the copyright occurs, certain advantages exist for publishing a work with notice.

Prior to March 1, 1989, the requirement for the notice applied equally whether the work was published in the United States or elsewhere by authority of the copyright owner. Compliance with the statutory notice requirements was the responsibility of the copyright owner. Unauthorized publication without the copyright notice, or with a defective notice, does not affect the validity of the copyright in the work.

Advance permission from, or registration with, the Copyright Office is not required before placing a copyright notice on copies of the work or on phonorecords of a sound recording. Moreover, for works first published on or after January 1, 1978, through February 28, 1989, omission of the required notice, or use of a defective notice, did not result in forfeiture or outright loss of copyright protection. Certain omissions of, or defects in, the notice of copyright, however, could have led to loss of copyright protection if steps were not taken to correct or cure the omissions or defects. The Copyright Office has issued a final regulation (37 CFR 201.20) that suggests various acceptable positions for the notice of copyright. For further information, write to the Copyright Office and request Circular 3, "Copyright Notice", and Circular 96, Section 201.20, "Methods of Affixation and Positions of the Copyright Notice on Various Types of Works."

Works Already in the Public Domain

Neither the 1976 Copyright Act, the Berne Convention Implementation Act of 1988, the Copyright Renewal Act of 1992, nor the Sonny Bono Copyright Term Extension Act of 1998 will restore protection to works that fell into the public domain before the passage of the laws. However, the North American Free Trade Agreement Implementation Act (NAFTA) and the Uruguay Round Agreements Act (URAA) may restore copyright in certain works of foreign origin that were in the public domain in the United States. Under the copyright law in effect prior to January 1, 1978, copyright could be lost in several situations. The most common were publication without the required notice of copyright, expiration of the first 28-year term without renewal, or final expiration of the second copyright term. The Copyright Renewal Act of 1992 automatically renews first term copyrights secured between January 1, 1964, and December 31, 1977.

Scope of Exclusive Rights Under Copyright

The present law has changed and enlarged in some cases the scope of the copyright owner's rights. The new rights apply to all uses of a work subject to protection by copyright after January 1, 1978, regardless of when the work was created.

———————— DURATION OF COPYRIGHT PROTECTION ————————

Works Originally Copyrighted On or After January 1, 1978

A work that is created and fixed in tangible form for the first time on or after January 1, 1978, is automatically protected from the moment of its creation and is ordinarily given a term enduring for the author's life plus an additional 70 years after the author's death. In the case of "a joint work prepared by two or more authors who did not work for hire," the term lasts for 70 years after the last surviving author's death. For works made for hire and for anonymous and pseudonymous works (unless the author's identity is revealed in the Copyright Office records), the duration of copyright will be 95 years from publication or 120 years from creation, whichever is less. Works created before the 1976 law came into effect but neither published nor registered for copyright before January 1, 1978, have been automatically brought under the statute and are now given federal copyright protection. The duration of copyright in these works will generally be computed in the same way as for new works: the life-plus-70 or 95/120-year terms will apply. However, all works in this category are guaranteed at least 25 years of statutory protection.

Works Copyrighted Before January 1, 1978

Under the law in effect before 1978, copyright was secured either on the date a work was published with notice of copyright or on the date of registration if the work was registered in unpublished form. In either case, copyright endured for a first term of 28 years from the date on which it was secured. During the last (28th) year of the first term, the copyright was eligible for renewal. The copyright law extends the renewal term from 28 to 67 years for copyrights in existence on January 1, 1978.

However, for works copyrighted prior to January 1, 1964, the copyright still must have been renewed in the 28th calendar year to receive the 67-year period of added protection. The amending legislation enacted June 26, 1992, automatically extends this second term for works first copyrighted between January 1, 1964, and December 31, 1977. For more detailed information on the copyright term, write or call the Copyright Office and request Circular 15a, "Duration of Copyright," and Circular 15t, "Extension of Copyright Terms."

———————————————————— WORKS FIRST PUBLISHED BEFORE 1978: THE COPYRIGHT NOTICE ————————————————————

GENERAL INFORMATION ABOUT THE COPYRIGHT NOTICE

In investigating the copyright status of works first published before January 1, 1978, the most important thing to look for is the notice of copyright. As a general rule under the previous law, copyright protection was lost permanently if the notice was omitted from the first authorized published edition of a work or if it appeared in the wrong form or position. The form and position of the copyright notice for various types of works were specified in the copyright statute. Some courts were liberal in overlooking relatively minor departures from the statutory requirements, but a basic failure to comply with the notice provisions forfeited copyright protection and put the work into the public domain in this country.

ABSENCE OF COPYRIGHT NOTICE

For works first published before 1978, the complete absence of a copyright notice from a published copy generally indicates that the work is not protected by copyright. For works first published before March 1, 1989, the copyright notice is mandatory, but omission could have been cured by registration before or within 5 years of publication and by adding the notice to copies published in the United States after discovery of the omission. Some works may contain a notice, others may not. The absence of a notice in works published on or after March 1, 1989, does not necessarily indicate that the work is in the public domain.

UNPUBLISHED WORKS. No notice of copyright was required on the copies of any unpublished work. The concept of "publication" is very technical, and it was possible for a number of copies lacking a copyright notice to be reproduced and distributed without affecting copyright protection.

FOREIGN EDITIONS. In the case of works seeking ad interim copyright [2], copies of a copyrighted work were exempted from the notice requirements if they were first published outside the United States. Some copies of these foreign editions could find their way into the United States without impairing the copyright.

ACCIDENTAL OMISSION. The 1909 statute preserved copyright protection if the notice was omitted by accident or mistake from a "particular copy or copies." Unauthorized Publication. A valid copyright was not secured if someone deleted the notice and/or published the work without authorization from the copyright owner.

SOUND RECORDINGS. Reproductions of sound recordings usually contain two different types of creative works: the underlying musical, dramatic, or literary work that is being performed or read and the fixation of the actual sounds embodying the performance or reading. For protection of the underlying musical or literary work embodied in a recording, it is not necessary that a copyright notice covering this material appear on the phonograph records or tapes on which the recording is reproduced. As noted above, a special notice is required for protection of the recording of a series of musical, spoken, or other sounds that were fixed on or after February 15, 1972. Sound recordings fixed before February 15, 1972, are not eligible for federal copyright protection. The Sound Recording Act of 1971, the present copyright law, and the Berne Convention Implementation Act of 1988 cannot be applied or be construed to provide any retroactive protection for sound recordings fixed before February 15, 1972. Such works, however, may be protected by various state laws or doctrines of common law.

THE DATE IN THE COPYRIGHT NOTICE

If you find a copyright notice, the date it contains may be important in determining the copyright status of the work. In general, the notice on works published before 1978 must include the year in which copyright was secured by publication or, if the work was first registered for copyright in unpublished form, the year in which registration was made. There are two main exceptions to this rule.

1. For pictorial, graphic, or sculptural works (Classes F through K under the 1909 law), the law permitted omission of the year date in the notice.

2. For "new versions" of previously published or copyrighted works, the notice was not usually required to include more than the year of first publication of the new version itself. This is explained further under "Derivative Works" below.

The year in the notice usually (though not always) indicated when the copyright began. It is, therefore, significant in determining whether a copyright is still in effect; or, if the copyright has not yet run its course, the year date will help in deciding when the copyright is scheduled to expire. For further information about the duration of copyright, request Circular 15a, "Duration of Copyright." In evaluating the meaning of the date in a notice, you should keep the following points in mind:

WORKS PUBLISHED AND COPYRIGHTED BEFORE JANUARY 1, 1978: A work published before January 1, 1978, and copyrighted within the past 75 years may still be protected by copyright in the United States if a valid renewal registration was made during the 28th year of the first term of the copyright. If renewed by registration or under the Copyright Renewal Act of 1992 and if still valid under the other provisions of the law, the copyright will expire 95 years from the end of the year in which it was first secured.

Therefore, the U.S. copyright in any work published or copyrighted prior to January 1, 1923, has expired by operation of law, and the work has permanently fallen into the public domain in the United States. For example, on January 1, 1997, copyrights in works first published or copyrighted before January 1, 1922, have expired; on January 1, 1998, copyrights in works first published or copyrighted before January 1, 1923, have expired. Unless the copyright law is changed again, no works under protection on January 1, 1999 will fall into the public domain in the United States until January 1, 2019.

WORKS FIRST PUBLISHED OR COPYRIGHTED BETWEEN JANUARY 1, 1923, AND DECEMBER 31, 1949, BUT NOT RENEWED:

If a work was first published or copyrighted between January 1, 1923, and December 31, 1949, it is important to determine whether the copyright was renewed during the last (28th) year of the first term of the copyright. This can be done by searching the Copyright Office records or catalogs as explained previously. If no renewal registration was made, copyright protection expired permanently at the end of the 28th year of the year date it was first secured.

WORKS FIRST PUBLISHED OR COPYRIGHTED BETWEEN JANUARY 1, 1923, AND DECEMBER 31, 1949, AND REGISTERED FOR RENEWAL: When a valid renewal registration was made and copyright in the work was in its second term on December 31, 1977, the renewal copyright term was extended under the latest act to 67 years. In these cases, copyright will last for a total of 95 years from the end of the year in which copyright was originally secured. Example: Copyright in a work first published in 1925 and renewed in 1953 will expire on December 31, 2020.

WORKS FIRST PUBLISHED OR COPYRIGHTED BETWEEN JANUARY 1, 1950, AND DECEMBER 31, 1963: If a work was in its first 28-year term of copyright protection on January 1, 1978, it must have been renewed in a timely fashion to have secured the maximum term of copyright protection. If renewal registration was made during the 28th calendar year of its first term, copyright would endure for 95 years from the end of the year copyright was originally secured. If not renewed, the copyright expired at the end of its 28th calendar year.

WORKS FIRST PUBLISHED OR COPYRIGHTED BETWEEN JANUARY 1, 1964, AND DECEMBER 31, 1977: If a work was in its first 28-year term of copyright protection on June 26, 1992, renewal registration is now optional. The term of copyright for works published or copyrighted during this time period has been extended to 95 years by the Copyright Renewal Act of 1992 and the Sonny Bono Term Extension Act of 1998. There is no need to make the renewal filing to extend the original 28-year copyright term to the full 95 years.

However, there are several advantages to making a renewal registration during the 28th year of the original term of copyright. If renewal registration is made during the 28th year of the original term of copyright, the renewal copyright vests in the name of the renewal claimant on the effective date of the renewal registration; the renewal certificate constitutes prima facie evidence as to the validity of the copyright during the renewed and extended term and of the facts stated in the certificate; and, the right to use the derivative work in the extended term may be affected. Request Circular 15, "Renewal of Copyright," for further information.

UNPUBLISHED, UNREGISTERED WORKS: Before 1978, if a work had been neither "published" in the legal sense nor registered in the Copyright Office, it was subject to perpetual protection under the common law. On January 1, 1978, all works of this kind, subject to protection by copyright, were automatically brought under the federal copyright statute. The duration of copyright for these works can vary, but none of them will expire before December 31, 2002.

DERIVATIVE WORKS

In examining a copy (or a record, disk, or tape) for copyright information, it is important to determine whether that particular version of the work is an original edition of the work or a "new version." New versions include musical arrangements, adaptations, revised or newly edited editions, translations, dramatizations, abridgments, compilations, and works republished with new matter added. The law provides that derivative works, published or unpublished, are independently copyrightable and that the copyright in such a work does not affect or extend the protection, if any, in the underlying work. Under the 1909 law, courts have also held that the notice of copyright on a derivative work ordinarily need not include the dates or other information pertaining to the earlier works incorporated in it. This principle is specifically preserved in the present copyright law. Thus, if the copy (or the record, disk, or tape) constitutes a derivative version of the work, these points should be kept in mind:

+ The date in the copyright notice is not necessarily an indication of when copyright in all the material in the work will expire. Some of the material may already be in the public domain, and some parts of the work may expire sooner than others.

+ Even if some of the material in the derivative work is in the public domain and free for use, this does not mean that the "new" material added to it can be used without permission from the owner of copyright in the derivative work. It may be necessary to compare editions to determine what is free to use and what is not.

+ Ownership of rights in the material included in a derivative work and in the preexisting work upon which it may be based may differ, and permission obtained from the owners of certain parts of the work may not authorize the use of other parts.

THE NAME IN THE COPYRIGHT NOTICE

Under the copyright statute in effect before 1978, the notice was required to include "the name of the copyright proprietor." The present act requires that the notice include "the name of the owner of copyright in the work, or an abbreviation by which the name can be recognized, or a generally known alternative designation of the owner." The name in the notice (sometimes in combination with the other statements on the copy, records, disk, tape, container, or label) often gives persons wishing to use the work the information needed to identify the owner from whom licenses or permission can be sought. In other cases, the name provides a starting point for a search in the Copyright Office records or catalogs, as explained at the beginning of this circular.

In the case of works published before 1978, copyright registration is made in the name of the individual person or the entity identified as the copyright owner in the notice. For works published on or after January 1, 1978, registration is made in the name of the person or entity owning all the rights on the date the registration is made. This may or may not be the name appearing in the notice. In addition to its records of copyright registration, the Copyright Office maintains extensive records of assignments, exclusive licenses, and other documents dealing with copyright ownership.

AD INTERIM

Ad interim copyright was a special short-term copyright that applied to certain books and periodicals in the English language that were first manufactured and published outside the United States. It was a partial exception to the manufacturing requirements of the previous U.S. copyright law. Its purpose was to secure temporary U.S. protection for a work, pending the manufacture of an edition in the United States. The ad interim requirements changed several times over the years and were subject to a number of exceptions and qualifications.

The manufacturing provisions of the copyright act expired on July 1, 1986, and are no longer a part of the copyright law. The transitional and supplementary provisions of the act provide that for any work in which ad interim copyright was subsisting or capable of being secured on December 31, 1977, copyright protection would be extended for a term compatible with the other works in which copyright was subsisting on the effective date of the new act.

Consequently, if the work was first published on or after July 1, 1977, and was eligible for ad interim copyright protection, the provisions of the present copyright act will be applicable to the protection of these works. Anyone investigating the copyright status of an English-language book or periodical first published outside the United States before July 1, 1977, should check carefully to determine:

+ Whether the manufacturing requirements were applicable to the work; and
+ If so, whether the ad interim requirements were met.
FOR FURTHER INFORMATION

Information via the Internet: Frequently requested circulars, announcements, regulations, other related materials, and all copyright application forms are available via the Internet. You may access these via the Copyright Office homepage at www.loc.gov/copyright.

Information by fax: Circulars and other information (but not application forms) are available by Fax-on-Demand at (202)707-2600.

Information by telephone: For general information about copyright, call the Copyright Public Information Office at (202)707-3000. The TTY number is (202)707-6737. Information specialists are on duty from 8:30 a.m. to 5:00 p.m., eastern time, Monday through Friday, except federal holidays. Recorded information is available 24 hours a day. Or, if you know which application forms and circulars you want, request them from the Forms and Publications Hotline at (202)707-9100 24 hours a day. Leave a recorded message.

Information by regular mail:
Write to:
Library of Congress
Copyright Office
Publications Section, LM-455
101 Independence Avenue, S.E.
Washington, D.C. 20559-6000
UNITED STATES COPYRIGHT OFFICE / THE LIBRARY OF CONGRESS

SEARCH REQUEST FORM

Library of Congress Copyright Office 101 Independence Avenue, S.E. Washington, D.C. 20559-6000

Reference & Bibliography Section (202) 707-6850 8:30 a.m. to 5 p.m., Monday through Friday, eastern time

Type of work:

Book Music Motion Picture Drama Sound Recording Computer Program Photograph/Artwork Map Periodical Contribution Architectural Work Mask Work

Search information you require: Registration Renewal Assignment Address

Specifics of work to be searched:
TITLE:
AUTHOR:
COPYRIGHT CLAIMANT (name in c notice):
APPROXIMATE YEAR DATE OF PUBLICATION/CREATION:
REGISTRATION NUMBER (if known):
OTHER IDENTIFYING INFORMATION:
If you need more space please attach additional pages.

——————————— Estimates are based on the Copyright Office fee of $65 [1] an hour or fraction of an hour consumed. The more information you furnish as a basis for the search, the better service we can provide. The time between the date of receipt of your fee for the search and your receiving a report will vary from 8 to 12 weeks depending on workload.

NAMES, TITLES, AND SHORT PHRASES ARE NOT COPYRIGHTABLE.

Please read Circular 22 for more information on copyright searches. ———

———————————————————————————————————————

YOUR NAME: DATE: ADDRESS: DAYTIME TELEPHONE NO.
(___) ___-____

Convey results of estimate/search by telephone yes no

Fee enclosed?   _ yes Amount $__________
                 _ no
——————— ENDNOTES

1 NOTE: Registration filing fees and search fees are effective through June 30, 2002. For information on the fee changes, please write the Copyright Office, check the Copyright Office Website at www.loc.gov/copyright, or call (202) 707-3000.

2 "Ad interim copyright" refers to a special short term of copyright available to certain pre-1978 books and periodicals. For further information on ad interim copyright, see page 10.

*****

[Federal Register: September 29, 1995 (Volume 60, Number 189)]
[Page 50414-50423]
[ML 509]

LIBRARY OF CONGRESS

Copyright Office

37 CFR Parts 201 and 202

[Docket No. 95-1B]

Restoration of Certain Berne and WTO Works

AGENCY: Copyright Office, Library of Congress.

ACTION: Final regulations

SUMMARY: The Copyright Office is issuing final regulations establishing procedures that govern the filing of Notices of Intent to Enforce copyright (NIEs) and the registering of copyright claims to restored works as required by the Uruguay Round Agreements Act. The Act automatically restores copyright for certain foreign works effective January 1, 1996. Although restoration is automatic, the copyright owner may file a Notice of Intent to Enforce the Restored Copyright with the Copyright Office in order to enforce rights against reliance parties.

EFFECTIVE DATE: These final regulations are effective October 1, 1995.

FOR FURTHER INFORMATION CONTACT: Marilyn J. Kretsinger, Acting General
Counsel, Copyright GC/I&R, P.O. Box 70400, Southwest Station, Washington, D.C. 20024. Telephone: (202) 707-8380. Telefax: (202) 707-8366.
I. Background

On December 8, 1994, President Clinton signed the "Uruguay Round Agreements Act" (URAA), Pub. L. No. 103-465, 108 Stat. 4809. The URAA contains several significant copyright amendments. It amends the software rental provision found in 17 U.S.C. 109(b) by eliminating the expiration or sunset date, amends Titles 17 and 18 to create civil and criminal remedies for "bootlegging" sound recordings of live musical performances and music videos, and adds a new 17 U.S.C. Sec. 104A which restores copyright in certain foreign works. The URAA also gives the Copyright Office several responsibilities related to restoration of those works.

A. Restoration of Copyright in Eligible Works

Under the URAA, restoration of copyright in works from countries which are currently eligible occurs automatically on January 1, 1996. An eligible country is a nation, other than the United States, that is a member of the Berne Convention, <SUP>1 or a member of

[[Page 50415]]

the World Trade Organization, or is the subject of a presidential proclamation declaring its eligibility.

\1\ Convention concerning the creation of an International Union for the Protection of Literary and Artistic Works (Sept. 9, 1886, revised in 1908, 1928, 1948, 1967, 1971), hereinafter cited as the Berne Convention.

Works from any source country eligible under the URAA may be subject to automatic copyright restoration. However, to be so restored, a work must meet certain other requirements:

1. It is not in the public domain in its source country through expiration of the term of protection;

2. It is in the public domain in the United States due to noncompliance with formalities imposed at any time by United States copyright law, lack of subject matter protection in the case of sound recordings fixed before February 15, 1972, or lack of national eligibility;

3. It has at least one author or rightholder who was, at the time the work was created, a national or domiciliary of an eligible country;

4. If published, it was first published in an eligible country and was not published in the United States during the 30-day period following publication in such eligible country.

Notwithstanding the fact that the work meets the above requirements, any work ever owned or administered by the Alien Property Custodian and in which the restored copyright would be owned by a government or instrumentality thereof, is not a restored work.

B. Effective Date of Restoration

Eligible copyrights are restored automatically on the date the Agreement on Trade Related Aspects of Intellectual Property (TRIPs) enters into force with respect to the United States (URAA, section 514(a)). As discussed in the Notice of Policy Decision and Public Meeting, the Copyright Office has concluded that the effective date of copyright restoration is January 1, 1996. 60 FR 7793 (Feb. 9, 1995). President Clinton has confirmed that the date on which the obligations of the TRIPs Agreement will take effect for the United States is January 1, 1996. Proclamation No. 6780, 60 FR 15845 (Mar. 27, 1995).

II. The Copyright Office's Responsibilities

Although copyright restoration is automatic for eligible works, the URAA charged the Office with establishing regulations to govern the filing of Notices of Intent to Enforce (NIEs) restored copyrights and the registering of copyright claims in restored works by no later than October 1, 1995.

The Act also requires the Office to publish a list in the Federal Register identifying restored works and their ownership where NIEs have been filed with the Office. The Office must also maintain a list containing all NIEs for inspection and copying by the public.

A. Notices of Intent To Enforce

1. Notification of Reliance Party

The URAA directs the owner of a restored work to notify reliance parties if the owner of the rights in a restored work plans to enforce those rights. A reliance party is typically a business or individual who, relying on the public domain status of a work, was already using the work prior to December 8, 1994, the date of enactment of the URAA. <SUP>2 The URAA authorizes the owner of a right in a restored work either to provide actual notice by serving a NIE directly on a reliance party or to provide constructive notice through the filing of a NIE with the Copyright Office.

\2\ This is true for the great majority of works. However, for works from any country which was not eligible under the URAA as of December 8, 1994, reliance parties would be those using the work before the date on which that country becomes an eligible country by joining Berne, the WTO, or as a result of a Presidential proclamation.

---

2. Effective Filing Date

A work whose source country is a member of the Berne Convention or the World Trade Organization on January 1, 1996, is restored on that date. The owner of such a work may file a NIE concerning that work between January 1, 1996, and December 31, 1997. The Office will publish the first listing of NIEs no later than May 1, 1996, and will publish lists at regular four-month intervals for a period of two years thereafter.

In the case of works from any source country which became eligible for restoration under the URAA after January 1, 1996, owners of such works may file NIEs with the Copyright Office for a two year period starting from the date that country became eligible. The Office will also publish a list of NIEs as detailed above, for works from any of those countries, but the time frame for such lists will be measured from the date a particular country becomes eligible.

3. Effect of Notice on Reliance Party

A reliance party has a twelve-month period to sell off previously manufactured stock, to publicly perform or display the work, or to authorize others to conduct these activities. This period begins when the owner of a restored work notifies the reliance party that the owner is enforcing copyright in the identified work. The date runs from either the date of publication in the Federal Register identifying the work or receipt of actual notice. If Notice of Intent to Enforce a Restored Copyright is provided both by publication in the Federal Register and service on the reliance party, the period runs from whichever date is the earlier, the date of Federal Register publication or service of actual notice. All reliance parties, except those who created certain derivative works, must cease using the work at the end of the twelve-month period unless they reach a licensing agreement with the copyright owner for continued use of the restored work.

B. Registration of Copyright Claims in Restored Works

The second filing that the owner of a restored work may choose to make with the Copyright Office is an application for registration of a copyright claim. Copyright registration is voluntary; the URAA directs the Office to have procedures for such registration, but it does not require owners of the restored works to register. Although the owner of a work not considered a Berne work as defined in 17 U.S.C. 101 must obtain or seek registration for a work before he or she can bring a copyright infringement action, the owner of rights in a Berne work does not have to register before initiating suit. [3]

\3\ It would seem that this exception would apply only to works that meet the definition of a ``Berne Convention work" in 17 U.S.C. 101.

It is true that the holder of a copyright certificate of registration may secure some procedural advantages in litigating a copyright suit based on the effective date of registration. If registration is made before or within 5 years of publication, it will establish prima facie evidence in court of the validity of the copyright and of the facts stated in the certificate; and if registration is made within 3 months after publication of the work or prior to an infringement of the work, statutory damages and attorney's fees will be available to the copyright owner in court actions. Otherwise, only an award of actual damages and profits is available to the copyright owner.

III. The Comments

A. Comments Submitted

The Copyright Office sought public comment concerning the implementation of the URAA both prior to and after publication of its Notice of Proposed Rulemaking (NPRM). The Office first published a notice inviting interested parties to submit written comments and/or to attend a public meeting held at the Copyright Office on March 20, 1995, to discuss issues

[[Page 50416]]

related to NIEs and registration of restored works. 60 FR 7793 (Feb. 9, 1995). The Office sent this notice to over ninety authors rights organizations and industry groups, as well as 182 foreign government agencies with copyright authority, to give them the opportunity to respond. Approximately forty individuals attended the meeting, including representatives from authors' rights organizations, museums, the publishing industry, the film industry, and the computer software industry. <SUP>4 Fifteen written comments were submitted. The Office considered all of these views as it developed proposed procedures for the filing of NIEs and the registering of copyright claims in restored works. On July 10, the Office published proposed regulations in the Federal Register. 60 FR 35522 (July 10, 1995).

\4\ A copy of all written comments and a summary of the meeting can be found in the Public Information Office of the Copyright Office, Room LM-401, James Madison Memorial Building, Washington, D.C.

In the Notice of Proposed Rulemaking, the Office invited interested parties to submit written comments on the proposed regulations. The Office received comments from the following parties: The Association of American Publishers (AAP); Irwin Karp; Janine Lorente, for Societe des Auteurs et Compositeurs Dramatiques (SACD); Nancy McAleer, for Thomson & Thomson; Bill Patry; David Pierce; Linda Shaughnessy, for AP Watt Ltd. Literary Agents; Ellen Theg, for International Television Trading Corp.; and Richard Wincor, of Coudert Brothers.
The Office notes that some of the comments received in response to the NPRM had already been addressed, and some called for minor clarifications that have been made to the final regulations. Other comments, whether raised for the first or second time, raise substantive issues that are discussed below.

B. Issues Related to Notices of Intent To Enforce

1. Formality

Ms. Shaughnessy stated that since copyright restoration is to occur automatically, the procedures for filing NIEs are exceptionally onerous. She asserted it should be sufficient to file one NIE for all of the titles of one author. Ms. Shaughnessy illustrated her point by noting that she will be filing for 73 authors, but there will be hundreds of titles involved. Comment 3. Ms. Lorente asserted that the NIE is a formality in violation of at least the spirit of Berne and that because reliance parties are free to continue to exploit restored works in the United States unless a NIE is filed, an author cannot exercise his or her rights in the restored work automatically. Comment 5, at 1.

The Copyright Office again emphasizes that the restoration of copyright in certain foreign works considered in the public domain in the United States creates a conflict between reliance parties' and copyright owners' legitimate concerns. Reliance parties have invested capital and labor in the lawful exploitation of public domain property; the sudden restoration of copyright divests them of these investments. Without some provision addressing this potential loss, there could be challenges based on the ``taking'' clause of the Fifth Amendment of the U.S. Constitution. On the other hand, it is important that the United States restore copyright protection in certain foreign works. The United States arguably failed to conform its law fully to the Berne Convention in 1989 when it declined to interpret Article 18(1) on restoration [5] as being mandatory. The U.S. Justice Department in its review of the URAA legislation concluded that under existing precedents interpreting the Fifth Amendment, the Notice of Intent to Enforce the Restored Copyright avoided an unconstitutional ``taking.'' [6] Thus, the Justice Department considered these provisions as critical.

\5\ This Convention shall apply to all works which, at the moment of its coming into force, have not yet fallen into the public domain in the country of origin through the expiry of the term of protection. Berne Convention art. 18(1)(Paris text).

\6\ See Memorandum from Chris Schroeder, Counsellor to the Assistant Attorney General, Office of Legal Counsel, United States Dept. of Justice to Ira S. Shapiro, General Counsel, USTR, on Whether Certain Copyright Provisions in the Draft Legislation to Implement the Uruguay Round of Multilateral Trade Negotiations Would Constitute a Taking Under the Fifth Amendment (July 29, 1994).

We believe that such a filing is not inconsistent with the Berne Convention because Article 18(3) [7] of the Berne Convention specifically permits member nations to determine ``conditions'' for applying the principles of restoration. Copyright restoration occurs automatically; the URAA merely creates a narrow set of conditions requiring notification to reliance parties. Moreover, the information sought on the NIEs is calculated to assist in the voluntary licensing of the restored work. The decision of Congress to enact these provisions is, therefore, supported by the legitimate interests of both reliance parties and copyright owners, by constitutional considerations, and by Article 18(3) of the Berne Convention.

\7\ The application of this principle shall be subject to any provisions contained in special conventions to that effect existing or to be concluded between countries of the Union. In the absence of such provisions, the respective countries shall determine, each in so far as it is concerned, the conditions of application of this principle. Berne Convention art. 18(3) (Paris text).

The Office has tried, however, to make the procedures for filing NIEs practical, realizing that too detailed requirements would burden the owner and that too general ones would serve neither the owner nor the user of the restored work.

The Office also notes that the URAA makes such filings less onerous by permitting the owner to notify all reliance parties of a restored work by filing in one central place, the Copyright Office. Only if the owner does not file with the Copyright Office within the appropriate time period, as detailed above, must the owner provide actual notice to each user of a restored work in order to enforce rights.

The Office is permitting an owner of multiple works to file one NIE if each work is identified by title, has the same author, is owned by the same identified copyright owner or owner of an exclusive right, and the rights owned are the same.

2. Effective Date

Mr. Patry stated that January 1, 1995, is the initial date of copyright restoration. Comment 2, at 1. Mr. Karp asserted that the effective date of 104(A) is December 8, 1994, but that first restoration of copyrights will occur on January 1, 1996. Comment 8, at 2. The Office reaffirms its recognition of January 1, 1996, as the effective date of initial copyright restoration. 3. Minor Errors or Omissions

Ms. Lorente noted that it is often impossible for foreign authors to know the English language title under which a work is being exploited, especially as it is often not a literal translation. She, therefore, asked that a NIE not be invalidated if it gives the literal translation of the foreign title, and later it is determined that the English language title under which the work is exploited is different from the one given in the NIE. Comment 5, at 2.

All information on the NIE other than the original title of the foreign work must be completed in English. The law requires that an English translation of a foreign title be given on the NIE; it does not specify that it be the English title under which the work was exploited.

The Copyright Office will record the NIE under the titles that are provided; ultimately only a court can determine the validity of a NIE. However, the Office believes that a reasonable construction of the statute's

[[Page 50417]]

requirements would permit good faith discrepancies in the English translation.

Furthermore, the URAA allows a party who has filed a NIE with the Copyright Office to correct minor errors or omissions by further notice at any time after the NIE is filed. The procedures and fees are the same for filing a NIE which corrects a previously filed NIE, except that the party making the correction should refer to previous NIE's volume and page number in the Copyright Office Documents Records, if known, on the corrected NIE.

4. Additional Information

The AAP asked the Office to require copyright owners to expand on the information contained in the NIEs, such as the format on which first the work was fixed (film, disk, etc.), contributors (editors, publishers, or director, animator, screenwriter, cinematographer, etc.) and for photographs, collections, etc. a description (material/ subjects, organization, and/or classification). The AAP also asked the Office to request an e-mail address, names and addresses of any agents, representatives, or collecting societies that can serve as licensing authorities. The AAP suggested that the Office consider incentives such as fee discounts, for those providing more complete information. Comment 7, at 6-8. Ms. Theg asked that the year of creation be included in the NIE instead of the year of publication, since she believed it to be more consistently available. Comment 9, at 2.

The Office has incorporated some of the AAP's suggestions into the NIE format and hopes it has struck an appropriate balance in its NIE by requesting information helpful to reliance parties, while not burdening the filer of the NIE with lengthy and detailed suggested information.

5. Accessible and Useful Public Record

The URAA requires the Copyright Office to publish the titles and owners of restored works in the Federal Register. Since publication in the Federal Register is costly and the parties indicated that such information would not be as accessible as information made available via the Internet, the Office is limiting the information published in the Federal Register to what the law requires. Much of the information contained in the NIE will be available on COPICS, the Copyright Office's automated database of registrations and recorded copyright transfers and other documents. These records may be accessed by the public on terminals in the Copyright Office at the Library of Congress and are also available via the Internet.

Since Internet access is not universal, Ms. Lorente asked that other means of getting information about NIEs, including written inquiries to the Copyright Office, should not be excluded. Comment 5, at 3. The AAP stated that it would be useful if the database could be searched in directories that listed all works restored in a particular country of origin. Comment 7, at 11. The AAP also asked that each work/ title be given in a separate entry in the database. Comment 7, at 9.

Traditional search methods will continue to be available; NIEs may be searched in the COPICS database under the name of the owner, the titles it contains, as well as the names of the authors, if given. Although the Office will not index works by country of origin in the COPICS database or provide separate entries in the database for multiple works listed on one NIE, each work can be easily identified since the database is searchable by title, author, and the owner or owner of an exclusive right.

Finally, though online access will be the primary means for providing this information to the public, upon request the Copyright Office staff will search the records at the rate of $20 for each hour or fraction thereof and furnish a written report. Search requests should be sent to the Reference and Bibliography Section, Copyright Office, Library of Congress, Washington, D.C. 20559-6000. In addition, individuals may come to the Office and do their own search free of charge.

6. Filing Fee

Ms. Lorente stated that restoration of copyright should be automatic, and without a fee, comment 5, at 3, and Ms. Shaughnessy asked that only one fee be charged for all the works of an author. Comment 3.

The Office notes that all of the works involved have been considered in the public domain in the United States. The URAA provides that restoration of eligible works is automatic, and a NIE may be filed directly on a reliance party. However, a notice which is effective against all reliance parties may be filed with the Copyright Office. The Office must examine and record that notice, issue an acknowledgement, create a catalog entry that includes among other things all the titles, publish the information in the Federal Register, and maintain the online catalog of the information. The URAA gives the Office authority to fix reasonable fees based on these costs.

The Office realizes that requiring a filing on each work of an author will be onerous and we will permit multiple works meeting the criteria described in our regulations to be filed on one notice for a lesser fee.

7. Acknowledgement

Ms. Lorente, Mr. Pierce and Ms. Theg all asserted that it is essential that the Copyright Office confirm the filing of a NIE. Ms. Lorente stated that it is very important that an author or agent have a document providing that he or she has complied with the URAA's provisions. See comment 5, at 2; comment 6, at 1; and comment 9, at 3. Ms. McAleer stressed that the acknowledgement of the recording of a NIE is an essential service because of the possibility that the NIE may be misplaced, causing its publication in the Federal Register to be delayed. Comment 4.

The Office will mail an acknowledgement of recordation to the filer of a NIE, including the date of receipt, the volume and page on which the NIE is recorded, and the anticipated date of publication in the Federal Register. The Office will not issue a certificate of recordation. Completed recordations will appear in the COPICS database and the Federal Register.

8. Transfers

Mr. Pierce asked that the Office require NIE filers, other than the author, to reference documents of transfer by date, parties and rights transferred, if any. He stated that this would decrease fraud and be less burdensome than filing the agreements with the Documents Unit of the Copyright Office. Comment 6, at 2.

While the Copyright Office agrees that such a requirement might be useful, it cannot adopt this requirement since it is not authorized by the URAA.

9. Federal Register Publication

The AAP agreed that, compared to the online database, the lists published in the Federal Register would be of secondary importance. AAP suggested, however, that the Federal Register entry also include the name of the author if possible. Comment 7, at 11.

In order to minimize costs, the Office has concluded that only the minimum information (title, name of the first owner or owner of an exclusive right identified on the NIE), will be included in the list of NIEs published in the Federal Register.

[[Page 50418]]

C. Issues Related to Registration of a Restored Work

1. Simultaneous Registration

Ms. Lorente asserted that registration is a second formality, and asked for simultaneous filing of NIEs and registration of copyright claims. She also argued both should be automatic and at no additional cost. Comment 5, at 2. Ms. Theg asked that the application for registration be modified to include the additional information requested in the NIE so that the NIE filing requirements could be satisfied at the time of making an application for registration. Comment 9, at 1.

As discussed earlier, procedures permitting the copyright registration of restored works are not formalities in violation of the Berne Convention. Registration is entirely voluntary for Berne works since copyright registration of restored works is not a prerequisite for the filing of a copyright infringement action. Registration of a claim in a work involves significant additional work and by law requires a fee. The Office has, however, attempted to keep the processing work and the fees to a minimum.

2. New URAA Related Registration Procedures

Mr. Pierce observed that registration, especially of motion pictures, is often very burdensome for foreign works, because of the difficulty in determining original publication dates and in submitting a copy of the work as first released. He concluded that applications will be filed for only a small percentage of the works unless the Office considers adopting more liberal deposit requirements such as accepting PAL, SECAM, VHS formats or written descriptions, allowing the registration of related works with multiple publication dates on one application, accepting approximate publication dates, and accepting a previously submitted deposit instead of requiring a new deposit. Comment 6, at 2. Ms. Theg asked that deposit requirements be waived entirely. Comment 9, at 2.

On the other side, the AAP questioned the necessity for changes in the existing registration and recordation systems. If such changes are made, the AAP asserted that they should not create precedent for other registration and deposit practices. The AAP also questioned the need for procedures allowing blanket exemptions in some instances for depositing materials, accepting descriptive materials instead of a copy of the work, and allowing certain collections such as photos or TV series to be given a single identifying group name or title. The AAP is concerned that these procedures will make it difficult for reliance parties to identify restored works and comply with the law. The AAP asked that the Office instead deal with special situations on a case- by-case basis. Comment 7, at 12-16.

The procedures developed for the registration of copyright claims for restored works must both balance the needs of applicants for copyright registration, reliance parties, the public, and the Copyright Office and also establish a system that will be feasible administratively and elicit necessary information. As indicated in our final regulations, these new procedures apply only to works restored under the URAA and NAFTA; they thus have no precedential effect on other filings.

3. Claimant for Registration

Mr. Patry noted that the applicable statutory language relating to the filing of NIEs permits the ``owners of restored copyright or the owner of an exclusive right therein'' to file a NIE, while the URAA statutory language covering registration indicates that ``owners of restored copyrights'' may apply for copyright registration. He asserted the statute's failure to mention the owner of an exclusive right in connection with registration means that only an author may file a registration. Comment 2, at 1-2.

The Office agrees that the restored copyright vests initially in the author as determined by the law of the source country of the work. A work, however, is registered in the name of a claimant. 17 U.S.C. 409. ``Claimant'' is a term of art defined in existing Copyright Office regulations, as either the author of a work or a person or organization that has obtained ownership of all rights under the copyright initially belonging to the author. 37 CFR 202.3(a)(3). Thus, an owner of only an exclusive right would not be permitted to file an application in his or her own name as the copyright claimant, although he or she could submit an application. While the URAA authorizes the Office to adopt regulations permitting owners of restored copyrights to file for registration of the restored copyright, there is nothing in the URAA to suggest that parties who register a restored work are any different from those under existing copyright law and regulations. Moreover, it seems essential to retain the concept of claimant since authors may no longer be alive.

4. Foreign Law

The AAP stated that since URAA registrations may create legal presumptions as to the validity of the copyright and the facts stated on the registration certificate, the Office should question an applicant's determination of foreign law issues. Comment 7, at 15. Mr. Karp asserted that since foreign law questions will arise with respect to many issues related to rights restored, including initial ownership, the Office should accept multiple NIEs or registrations for the same work. Comment 8, at 2.

The Copyright Office will accept such multiple, and possibly adverse, NIEs and registrations for the same work. One of the more difficult issues facing the Office is to what extent foreign law issues should be raised in the registration process. Section 104A(b) of the Act provides: ``A restored work vests initially in the author or initial rightholder of the work as determined by the law of the source country of the work.'' Determining the appropriate source country and the applicable foreign law is a question that must ultimately be resolved by a court. At most, the Office could simply question whether or not an author was in fact the author under the law of the source country. The applicant's answer would have to be accepted. The Office does not, therefore, plan to question an applicant's determination of foreign law issues.

IV. Procedures for Notices of Intent To Enforce

A Copyright Office task force has been meeting for several months to discuss issues related to establishing regulations for URAA filings. The Office also carefully considered the comments made at the public meeting and those submitted by interested parties in response to the Notice of Policy Decision and Public Meeting and the Notice of Proposed Rulemaking. Most of the commentators supported a detailed NIE rather than one limited to the minimal information required by the statute. Based on those comments, the Office is requesting more information from the filer of a NIE than required under the URAA. As provided in the statute, this additional information will not affect the validity of the notice. Additional information such as the identity of the author is essential, however, for efficient and timely identification of a specific work where enforcement of copyright is sought. The additional information will also facilitate the licensing of uses of restored works. Therefore, the Office urges those parties who are filing NIEs to provide as much of this additional information as possible.

[[Page 50419]]

A. Format for NIEs

1. Constructive Notice

The Copyright Office will not publish NIE forms; however, a suggested format for NIEs to be filed with the Office is included in the Appendix below. This format is available over the Internet and can be downloaded for use as a form. The suggested format requests information required by the statute and optional information which is extremely useful.

2. Actual Notice

Those parties choosing to serve actual Notice of Intent to Enforce a Restored Copyright on the reliance party should note that the URAA requires additional information. Therefore, if they use the Copyright Office's NIE format as a guide for the actual notice, it will be incomplete unless the additional information specified is added. The URAA specifies:

Notices of Intent to Enforce a Restored Copyright served on a reliance party shall be signed by the owner or the owner's agent, shall identify the restored work and the work in which the restored work is used, if any, in detail sufficient to identify them, include an English translation of the title, any other alternative titles known to the owner by which the work may be identified, the use or uses to which the owner objects, and an address and telephone number at which the reliance party may contact the owner. If the notice is signed by an agent, the agency relationship must have been constituted in writing and signed by the owner before service of the notice.[8]

62

\8\ Emphasis added to show additional requirements for actual notice.

104A(e)(2)(B) of the URAA. Actual notices may be served on a reliance party at any time after the work is restored.

3. Who may file a Notice of Intent To Enforce?

A NIE may be filed by someone who has the authority to sign it. The statute says that the NIE must be signed by the owner or the owner's agent. It can also be signed by the owner of any exclusive right in the restored copyright. As noted in the URAA and emphasized in the certification requirement, an agent cannot sign a NIE unless the agency relationship was constituted in writing signed by the owner before the notice is filed. 104A(e)(1)(A)(i) of the URAA.

B. Filing Fee

The filing fee is 30 U. S. dollars [9] for a NIE covering one work; for a NIE covering multiple works the fee is $30 for the first work, plus one dollar for each additional work. This fee includes the cost of an acknowledgement of recordation which will be mailed to the filer after the Copyright Office records the NIE. The regulations provide special instructions for payment of the filing fee, including payment by credit card. These instructions must be followed in order to permit processing of the fee. In addition, the filer of a NIE must insure that sufficient funds are available for payment. Insufficient fees could delay the effective date of notice.

\9\ All references to charges will be in terms of U.S. dollars.

For all URAA filings, both recordation of a NIE and registration of a restored work, the Copyright Office will accept Visa and MasterCard and American Express credit cards to facilitate payment in U.S. dollars. Payment by credit card is, however, available only for URAA filings.[10]

\10\ Acceptance of credit cards for URAA filings will serve as a test, however, by which the Office can determine at a later date the feasibility of accepting credit cards for other registrations and recordations.

C. Certification

The Office requires the filer of a NIE to sign a certification statement at the end of the document filed indicating that the information given is correct to the best of his or her knowledge. The URAA explicitly states that any materially false statement knowingly made with respect to any restored copyright identified in any Notice of Intent shall make void all claims and assertions made with respect to such restored copyright. 104A(e)(3) of the URAA.

D. Mailing Address

Time is critical with processing NIEs, and it is, therefore, important that URAA mail not come in with regular Copyright Office mail. All NIEs should be mailed to: URAA/GATT, NIEs and Registrations, P.O. Box 72400, Southwest Station, Washington, D.C. 20024, USA.

V. Procedures for Registering Copyright Claims in Restored Works

The URAA raises a number of unique considerations regarding the registration of copyright claims in restored works. First, a number of technical requirements, many of which are contained in the definition of ``restored work,'' govern whether a foreign work is subject to automatic restoration under the URAA. In many cases applicants seeking registration will be foreign claimants who are unfamiliar with the registration procedures in the United States Copyright Office. In addition, communication over technical issues may be difficult. Finally, virtually all of the restored copyrights will be older works; and in some cases, submitting a copy or phonorecord of the work will be a problem.

The Copyright Office weighed all of these considerations before developing a procedure for registering copyright claims in restored works. The Office has adopted a simplified procedure, which will still maintain the integrity of the public record and adhere to the provisions of the existing copyright law and the URAA.

The Office will register a claim to United States copyright in any work for which copyright protection is restored by the URAA, even if a registration was previously made before the work entered the public domain in this country. The Office will also register a claim for any work previously registered where the Office originally advised the copyright claimant that there was some doubt concerning compliance with the formal requirements of the law.

A. Registration Forms

Because the URAA creates unique eligibility requirements, the Copyright Office concluded that it should create two new registration forms and a continuation page specifically designed to obtain the information necessary for a GATT registration made under the URAA. They are Form GATT, Form GATT/GRP and Form GATT/CON. The Form GATT covers registration of individual restored works and restored works published under a single series title, Form GATT/GRP covers registration of groups of related restored works under the conditions set forth in the regulations, and the Form GATT/CON is a page providing additional space and may be used with either of the GATT application forms.

B. Deposit Required

In recognition of the difficulty some applicants may have in submitting a deposit of an older work ``as first published,'' the Office has established special deposit regulations for URAA restored works. These regulations permit a deposit of other than the first published edition of the work, if absolutely necessary; applicants should keep in mind, however, that the deposit serves as a crucial part of the public record, and it is their interest to make a complete deposit.

C. Filing Fee

The filing fee for registration is $20, since the Copyright Office believes the work in administering the registration procedure for restored works will be roughly comparable to general

[[Page 50420]]

registration procedures. In addition, the regulations contain special group registration options which will permit the registration of:

(1) A group of works published under a single series title. Form GATT should be used; the fee is $20 for up to a calendar year's worth of episodes, installments, or issues published under the same single series title; and

(2) A group of at least two, but up to ten related individual works published within the same calendar year. Form GATT/GRP should be used, the fee is ten dollars per individual work, that is between $20-$100 per application.

The registration regulations contain special instructions for payment of the filing fee, including payment by credit card.

D. Mailing Address

All GATT/URAA applications for registration should be mailed to: URAA/GATT, NIEs and Registrations, P.O. Box 72400, Southwest Station, Washington, DC 20024, USA.
VI. NAFTA

Exactly a year before the URAA was signed into law, Congress enacted the North American Free Trade Agreement Implementation Act (NAFTA) of December 8, 1993, adding a new section 104A to the Copyright Code that allowed copyright restoration in certain Mexican and Canadian works. See generally, Federal Register notices leading to the implementation of NAFTA, 59 FR 1408 (Jan. 10, 1994); 59 FR 12162 (Mar. 16, 1994); and 59 FR 58787 (Nov. 15, 1994). Although Congress modeled the URAA provisions on NAFTA, there are significant differences. For example, under the URAA, copyright restoration is automatic; under NAFTA it was not. Moreover, the URAA requires an English translation of the title as part of the NIE, but NAFTA did not require an English translation for NAFTA statements of intent.

In enacting these two laws, Congress intended the restoration provisions to operate separately from one another. Therefore, works restored under NAFTA are not additionally restored under the URAA. It is clear that Congress intended a new section 104A enacted in the URAA, to replace the NAFTA version of section 104A. Unfortunately, the statutory language in the URAA creates some ambiguities. The recent presidential proclamation clarifies some of these questions. 60 FR 15845 (Mar. 27, 1995).

The regulation governing filings under NAFTA will be amended to reflect a reference to the public law. This change is made necessary by the deletion of the NAFTA version of section 104A. In addition, Secs. 201.33 and 202.12 of the Copyright Office regulations contain provisions clarifying that works already restored under NAFTA do not additionally fall within the provisions of the URAA.

Despite the differences in NAFTA and URAA notice filings, the registration procedures, including deposit preferences, available for URAA restored works are also available for those works restored under NAFTA.

List of Subjects

37 CFR Part 201

Cable television, Copyright, Jukeboxes, Literary works, Satellites.

37 CFR Part 202

Claims, Copyright.

In consideration of the foregoing, the Copyright Office amends 37
CFR parts 201 and 202 in the manner set forth below:
PART 201—GENERAL PROVISIONS

1. The authority citation for part 201 is revised to read as follows:

Authority: 17 U.S.C. 702.

2. Section 201.31 is amended by revising the first sentence of paragraph (a) to
read as follows:

Sec. 201.31 Procedures for copyright restoration in the United States for
certain motion pictures and their contents in accordance with the North
American Free Trade Agreement.

(a) General. This section prescribes the procedures for submission of
Statements of Intent pertaining to the restoration of copyright protection in
the United States for certain motion pictures and works embodied therein as
required by the North American Free Trade Agreement Implementation Act
of December 8, 1993, Public Law No. 103-182. * * *

* * * * *

3. Section 201.33 is added to read as follows:

Sec. 201.33 Procedures for filing Notices of Intent to Enforce a restored
copyright under the Uruguay Round Agreements Act.

(a) General. This section prescribes the procedures for submission of Notices
of Intent to Enforce a Restored Copyright under the Uruguay Round
Agreements Act, as required in 17 U.S.C. 104A(a). On or before May 1, 1996,
and every four months thereafter, the Copyright Office will publish in the

Federal Register a list of works for which Notices of Intent to Enforce have been filed. It will maintain a list of these works. The Office will also make a more complete version of the information contained in the Notice of Intent to Enforce available on its automated database, which can be accessed over the Internet.

(b) Definitions—(1) NAFTA work means a work restored to copyright on January 1, 1995, as a result of compliance with procedures contained in the North American Free Trade Agreement Implementation Act of December 8, 1993, Public Law No. 103-182.

(2) Reliance party means any person who—

(i) With respect to a particular work, engages in acts, before the source country of that work becomes an eligible country under the URAA, which would have violated 17 U.S.C. 106 if the restored work had been subject to a copyright protection and who, after the source country becomes an eligible country, continues to engage in such acts;

(ii) Before the source country of a particular work becomes an eligible country, makes or acquires one or more copies of phonorecords of that work; or

(iii) As the result of the sale or other disposition of a derivative work, covered under the new 17 U.S.C. 104A(d)(3), or of significant assets of a person, described in the new 17 U.S.C. 104 A(d)(3) (A) or (B), is a successor, assignee or licensee of that person.

(3) Restored work means an original work of authorship that—

(i) Is protected under 17 U.S.C. 104A(a);

(ii) Is not in the public domain in its source country through expiration of term of protection;

(iii) Is in the public domain in the United States due to—

(A) Noncompliance with formalities imposed at any time by United States copyright law, including failure of renewal, lack of proper notice, or failure to comply with any manufacturing requirements;

(B) Lack of subject matter protection in the case of sound recordings fixed before February 15, 1972; or

(C) Lack of national eligibility; and

(iv) Has at least one author or rightholder who was, at the time the work was created, a national or domiciliary of an eligible country, and if published, was first published in an eligible country and not published in the United States during the 30-day period following publication in such eligible country.

(4) Source country of a restored work is—

(i) A nation other than the United States; and

[[Page 50421]]

(ii) In the case of an unpublished work—

(A) The eligible country in which the author or rightholder is a national or domiciliary, or, if a restored work has more than one author or rightholder, the majority of foreign authors or rightholders are nationals or domiciliaries of eligible countries; or

(B) If the majority of authors or rightholders are not foreign, the nation other than the United States which has the most significant contacts with the work; and

(iii) In the case of a published work—

(A) The eligible country in which the work is first published; or

(B) If the restored work is published on the same day in two or more eligible countries, the eligible country which has the most significant contacts with the work.

(c) Forms. The Copyright Office does not provide forms for Notices of Intent to Enforce filed with the Copyright Office. It requests that filers of such notices follow the format set out in Appendix A of this section and give all of the information listed in paragraph (d) of this section. Notices of Intent to Enforce must be in English, and should be typed or printed by hand legibly in dark, preferably black, ink, on 8 1/2 by 11 inch white paper of good quality, with at least a one inch (or three cm) margin.

(d) Requirements for Notice of Intent to Enforce a Copyright Restored Under the Uruguay Round Agreements Act. (1) Notices of Intent to Enforce should be sent to the following address: URAA/GATT, NIEs and Registrations, P.O. Box 72400, Southwest Station, Washington, DC 20024, USA.

(2) The document should be clearly designated as ``Notice of Intent to Enforce a Copyright Restored under the Uruguay Round Agreements Act''.

(3) Notices of Intent to Enforce must include:

(i) Required information:

   (A) The title of the work, or if untitled, a brief description of
the work;
   (B) An English translation of the title if title is in a foreign
language;
(C) Alternative titles if any;

   (D) Name of the copyright owner of the restored work, or of an
owner of an exclusive right therein;
   (E) The address and telephone number where the owner of copyright
or the exclusive right therein can be reached; and
(F) The following certification signed and dated by the owner of copyright, or
the owner of an exclusive right therein, or the owner's authorized agent:

I hereby certify that for each of the work(s) listed above, I am the copyright owner, or the owner of an exclusive right, or the owner's authorized agent, the agency relationship having been constituted in a writing signed by the owner before the filing of this notice, and that the information given herein is true and correct to the best of my knowledge.

Signature——
—————————

Name (printed or typed)——————————————————————————————

As agent for (if applicable)—————————————————————————————

Date:——————————————————————————————————————

(ii) Optional but essential information:

(A) Type of work (painting, sculpture, music, motion picture, sound recording, book, etc.);

(B) Name of author(s);

(C) Source country;

(D) Approximate year of publication;

(E) Additional identifying information (e.g. for movies: director, leading actors, screenwriter, animator; for photographs or books: subject matter; for books: editor, publisher, contributors);

(F) Rights owned by the party on whose behalf the Notice of Intent to Enforce is filed (e.g., the right to reproduce/distribute/publicly display/publicly perform the work, or to prepare a derivative work based on the work, etc.); and

(G) Telefax number at which owner, exclusive rights holder, or agent thereof can be reached.

(4) Notices of Intent to Enforce may cover multiple works provided that each work is identified by title, all the works are by the same author, all the works are owned by the identified copyright owner or owner of an exclusive right, and the rights owned by the party on whose behalf the Notice of Intent is filed are the same. In the case of Notices of Intent to Enforce covering multiple works, the notice must separately designate for each work covered the title of the work, or if untitled, a brief description of the work; an English translation of the title if the title is in a foreign language; alternative titles, if any; the type of work; the source country; the approximate year of publication; and additional identifying information.

(5) Notices of Intent to Enforce works restored on January 1, 1996, may be submitted to the Copyright Office on or after January 1, 1996, through December 31, 1997.

(e) Fee.

(1) Amount. The filing fee for recording Notices of Intent to Enforce is 30 U.S. dollars for notices covering one work. For notices covering multiple works as described in paragraph (d)(4) of this section, the fee is 30 U.S. dollars, plus one dollar for each additional work covered beyond the first designated

work. For example, the fee for a Notice of Intent to Enforce covering three works would be $32. This fee includes the cost of an acknowledgement of recordation.

(2) Method of Payment. (i) Checks, money orders, or bank drafts. The Copyright Office will accept checks, money orders, or bank drafts made payable to the Register of Copyrights. Remittances must be redeemable without service or exchange fees through a United States institution, must be payable in United States dollars, and must be imprinted with American Banking Association routing numbers. International money orders, and postal money orders that are negotiable only at a post office are not acceptable. CURRENCY WILL NOT BE ACCEPTED.

(ii) Copyright Office Deposit Account. The Copyright Office maintains a system of Deposit Accounts for the convenience of those who frequently use its services. The system allows an individual or firm to establish a Deposit Account in the Copyright Office and to make advance deposits into that account. Deposit Account holders can charge copyright fees against the balance in their accounts instead of sending separate remittances with each request for service. For information on Deposit Accounts please write: Copyright Office, Library of Congress, Washington, DC 20559-6000, and request a copy of Circular 5, ``How to Open and Maintain a Deposit Account in the Copyright Office."

(iii) Credit cards. For URAA filings the Copyright Office will accept VISA and MasterCard. Debit cards cannot be accepted for payment. With the NIE, a filer using a credit card must submit a separate cover letter stating the name of the credit card, the credit card number, the expiration date of the credit card, the total amount, and a signature authorizing the Office to charge the fees to the account. To protect the security of the credit card number, the filer must not write the credit card number on the Notice of Intent to Enforce.

(f) Public online access.

(1) Almost all of the information contained in the Notice of Intent to Enforce is available online in the Copyright Office History Documents (COHD) file through the Library of Congress electronic information system LC MARVEL through the Internet. Except on Federal holidays, this information may be obtained on terminals in the Copyright Office at the Library of Congress Monday through Friday 8:30 a.m. - 5:00 p.m. U.S. Eastern Time or over the Internet Monday - Friday 6:30 a.m. - 9:30 p.m. U.S. Eastern

[[Page 50422]]

Time, Saturday 8:00 a.m. - 5 p.m., and Sunday 1:00 p.m. - 5:00 p.m.

(2) Alternative ways to connect through Internet are: (i) use the Copyright Office Home Page on the World Wide Web at: http://lcweb.loc.gov/copyright, (ii) telnet to locis.loc.gov or the numeric address 140.147.254.3, or (iii) telnet to marvel.loc.gov, or the numeric address 140.147.248.7 and log in as marvel, or (iv) use a Gopher Client to connect to marvel.loc.gov.

(3) Information available online includes: the title or brief description if untitled; an English translation of the title; the alternative titles if any; the name of the copyright owner or owner of an exclusive right; the author; the type of work; the date of receipt of the NIE in the Copyright Office; the date of publication in the Federal Register; the rights covered by the notice; and the address, telephone and telefax number (if given) of the copyright owner.

(4) Online records of Notices of Intent to Enforce are searchable by the title, the copyright owner or owner of an exclusive right, and the author.

(g) NAFTA work. The copyright owner of a work restored under NAFTA by the filing of a NAFTA Statement of Intent to Restore with the Copyright Office prior to January 1, 1995, is not required to file a Notice of Intent to Enforce under this regulation.

Appendix A to Sec. 201.33—Notice of Intent To Enforce a Copyright
Restored Under the Uruguay Round Agreements Act (URAA)
1. Title:————————————————————————————————

    (If this work does not have a title, state ``No title.'') OR
    Brief description of work (for untitled works only):

——

2. English translation of title (if applicable):————————————

3. Alternative title(s) (if any):————————————————————

4. Type of work:————————————————————————————

(e.g. painting, sculpture, music, motion picture, sound recording, book)

5. Name of author(s):————————————————————————————

6. Source country:————————————————————————————

7. Approximate year of publication:————————————————

8. Additional identifying information:————————————————

   (e.g. for movies; director, leading actors, screenwriter, animator,
   for photographs: subject matter; for books; editor, publisher,
contributors, subject matter).
9. Name of copyright owner:————————————————————

(Statements may be filed in the name of the owner of the restored copyright
or the owner of an exclusive right therein.) 10. If you are not the owner of all
rights, specify the rights you own:

————————————————————————————————————

(e.g. the right to reproduce/distribute publicly display/ publicly perform the
work, or to prepare a derivative work based on the work)

11. Address at which copyright owner may be contacted:

————————————————————————————————————

————————————————————————————————————

   (Give the complete address, including the country and an
``attention" line, or ``in care of" name, if necessary.)

12. Telephone number of owner:————————————————————

13. Telefax number of owner:——————————————————————

14. Certification and Signature:

I hereby certify that, for each of the work(s) listed above, I am the copyright
owner, or the owner of an exclusive right, or the owner's authorized agent, the
agency relationship having been constituted in a writing signed by the owner
before the filing of this notice, and that the information given herein is true
and correct to the best of my knowledge.

Signature:————————————————————————————————

Name (printed or typed):——————————————————————

As agent for (if applicable):——————————————————

Date:————————————————————————————————————

Note: Notices of Intent to Enforce must be in English, except for the original title, and either typed or printed by hand legibly in dark, preferably black, ink. They should be on 8 1/2" by 11" white paper of good quality, with at least a 1-inch (or 3 cm) margin.

PART 202—REGISTRATION OF CLAIMS TO COPYRIGHT

4. The authority citation for part 202 is revised to read as follows:

Authority: 17 U.S.C. 702.

5. A new Sec. 202.12 is added to read as follows:

Sec. 202.12 Restored copyrights.

(a) General. This section prescribes rules pertaining to the registration of foreign copyright claims which have been restored to copyright protection under section 104A of 17 U.S.C., as amended by the Uruguay Round Agreements Act, Public Law 103-465.

(b) Definitions. (1) For the purposes of this section, restored work and source country, have the definition given in the URAA and Sec. 201.33(b) of this chapter.

(2) Descriptive statement for a work embodied solely in machine- readable format is a separate written statement giving the title of the work, nature of the work (for example: computer program, database, videogame, etc.), plus a brief description of the contents or subject matter of the work.

(c) Registration. (1) General. Application, deposit, and filing fee for registering a copyright claim in a restored work under section 104A, as amended, may be submitted to the Copyright Office on or after January 1, 1996. The application, filing fee, and deposit should be sent in a single package to the following address: URAA/GATT, NIEs and Registration, P.O. Box 72400, Southwest Station, Washington, DC 20024, USA.

(2) GATT Forms. Application for registration for single works restored to copyright protection under URAA should be made on Form GATT. Application for registration for a group of works published under a single series title and published within the same calendar year should also be made on Form GATT. Application for a group of at least two and up to ten individual and related works as described in paragraph (c)(5)(ii) of this section should be made on Form GATT/GRP. GATT/URAA forms may be obtained by writing or calling the Copyright Office Hotline at (202) 707-9100. In addition, legible photocopies of these forms are acceptable if reproduced on good quality, 8\1/2\ by 11 inch white paper, and printed head to head so that page two is printed on the back of page one.

(3) Fee.

(i) Amount. The filing fee for registering a copyright claim in a restored work is 20 U.S. dollars. The filing fee for registering a group of multiple episodes under a series title under paragraph (c)(5)(i) of this section is also $20. The filing fee for registering a group of related works under paragraph (c)(5)(ii) of this section is 10 U.S. dollars per individual work.

(ii) Method of payment.

(A) Checks, money orders, or bank drafts. The Copyright Office will accept checks, money orders, or bank drafts made payable to the Register of Copyrights. Remittances must be redeemable without service or exchange fees through a United States institution, must be payable in United States dollars, and must be imprinted with American Banking Association routing numbers. In addition, international money orders, and postal money orders that are negotiable only at a post office are not acceptable. CURRENCY WILL NOT BE ACCEPTED.

(B) Copyright Office Deposit Account. The Copyright Office maintains a system of Deposit Accounts for the convenience of those who frequently use its services. The system allows an individual or firm to establish a Deposit Account in the Copyright Office and to make advance deposits into that account. Deposit Account holders can charge copyright fees against the balance in their accounts instead of sending separate remittances with each request for service. For information on Deposit Accounts please write: Register of Copyrights, Copyright Office, Library of Congress, Washington,

DC 20559, and request a copy of Circular 5, ``How to Open and Maintain a Deposit Account in the Copyright Office."

(C) Credit cards. For URAA registrations the Copyright Office will accept VISA and MasterCards, and American Express. Debit cards cannot be accepted for payment. With the registration

[[Page 50423]]

application, an applicant using a credit card must submit a separate cover letter stating the name of the credit card, the credit card number, the expiration date of the credit card, the total amount authorized and a signature authorizing the Office to charge the fees to the account. To protect the security of the credit card number, the applicant must not write the credit card number on the registration application.

(4) Deposit.

(i) General. The deposit for a work registered as a restored work under the amended section 104A, except for those works listed in paragraphs (c)(4)(ii) through (iv) of this section, should consist of one copy or phonorecord which best represents the copyrightable content of the restored work. In descending order of preference, the deposit should be:

(A) The work as first published;

(B) A reprint or re-release of the work as first published;

(C) A photocopy or identical reproduction of the work as first published; or

(D) A revised version which includes a substantial amount of the copyrightable content of the restored work with an indication in writing of the percentage of the restored work appearing in the revision.

(ii) Previously registered works. No deposit is needed for works previously registered in the Copyright Office.

(iii) Works embodied solely in machine-readable format. For works embodied only in machine-readable formats, the deposit requirements are as follows:

(A) One machine-readable copy and a descriptive statement of the work; or

(B) Representative excerpts of the work, such as printouts; or, if the claim extends to audiovisual elements in the work, a videotape of what appears on the screen.

(iv) Pictorial, graphic and sculptural works. With the exception of 3-dimensional works of art, the general deposit preferences specified under paragraph (c)(4)(i) of this section shall govern. For 3- dimensional works of art, the preferred deposit is one or more photographs of the work, preferably in color.

(v) Special relief. An applicant who is unable to submit any of the preferred deposits may seek an alternative deposit under special relief (37 CFR 202.20(d)). In such a case, the applicant should indicate in writing why the deposit preferences cannot be met, and submit alternative identifying materials clearly showing some portion of the copyrightable contents of the restored work which is the subject of registration.

(vi) Motion pictures. If the deposit is a film print (16 or 35 mm), the applicant should contact the Performing Arts Section of the Examining Division for delivery instructions. The telephone number is: (202) 707-6040; the telefax number is: (202) 707-1236.

(5) Group registration. Copyright claims in more than one restored work may be registered as a group in the following circumstances:

(i) Single series title. Works published under a single series title in multiple episodes, installments, or issues during the same calendar year may be registered as a group, provided the owner of U.S. rights is the same for all episodes, installments, or issues. The Form GATT should be used and the number of episodes or installments should be indicated in the title line. The filing fee for registering a group of such works is $20. In general, the deposit requirements applicable to restored works will be applied to the episodes or installments in a similar fashion. In the case of a weekly or daily television series, applicants should first contact the Performing Arts Section of the Examining Division. The telephone number is (202) 707-6040; the telefax number is (202) 707-1236. (ii) Group of related works. A group of related works may be registered on the Form GATT/GRP, provided the following conditions are met: the author(s) is the same for all works in the group; the owner of all United States rights is the same for all works in the group; all works must have been published in the same calendar year; all works fit within the same subject matter category, i.e., literary works, musical works, motion pictures, etc.; and there are at least two and not more than ten individual works in the group submitted. Applicants registering a group of related works must file for registration on the Form GATT/GRP. The filing fee for registering a group of related works is ten dollars per individual work.

(d) Works excluded. Works which are not copyrightable subject matter under title 17 of the U.S. Code, other than sound recordings fixed before February 15, 1972, shall not be registered as restored copyrights.

Dated: September 25, 1995.

Marybeth Peters,
Register of Copyrights.
Approved by:
James H. Billington,
The Librarian of Congress.
[FR Doc. 95-24244 Filed 9-28-95; 8:45 am]

9/29/95

*****

U.S. Copyright Office, WIPO Copyright Treaty

WIPO COPYRIGHT TREATY adopted by the Diplomatic Conference on December 20, 1996

Contents

Preamble
Article 1: Relation to the Berne Convention
Article 2: Scope of Copyright Protection
Article 3: Application of Articles 2 to 6 of the Berne Convention
Article 4: Computer Programs
Article 5: Compilations of Data (Databases)
Article 6: Right of Distribution
Article 7: Right of Rental
Article 8: Right of Communication to the Public
Article 9: Duration of the Protection of Photographic Works
Article 10: Limitations and Exceptions
Article 11: Obligations concerning Technological Measures
Article 12: Obligations concerning Rights Management Information
Article 13: Application in Time

Preamble

The Contracting Parties,

Desiring to develop and maintain the protection of the rights of authors in their literary and artistic works in a manner as effective and uniform as possible,

Recognizing the need to introduce new international rules and clarify the interpretation of certain existing rules in order to provide adequate solutions to the questions raised by new economic, social, cultural and technological developments,

Recognizing the profound impact of the development and convergence of information and communication technologies on the creation and use of literary and artistic works,

Emphasizing the outstanding significance of copyright protection as an incentive for literary and artistic creation,

Recognizing the need to maintain a balance between the rights of authors and the larger public interest, particularly education, research and access to information, as reflected in the Berne Convention,

Have agreed as follows:

Article 1

Relation to the Berne Convention

(1) This Treaty is a special agreement within the meaning of Article 20 of the Berne Convention for the Protection of Literary and Artistic Works, as regards Contracting Parties that are countries of the Union established by that Convention. This Treaty shall not have any connection with treaties other than the Berne Convention, nor shall it prejudice any rights and obligations under any other treaties.

(2) Nothing in this Treaty shall derogate from existing obligations that Contracting Parties have to each other under the Berne Convention for the Protection of Literary and Artistic Works.

(3) Hereinafter, "Berne Convention" shall refer to the Paris Act of July 24, 1971 of the Berne Convention for the Protection of Literary and Artistic Works.

(4) Contracting Parties shall comply with Articles 1 to 21 and the Appendix of the Berne Convention.

Article 2

Scope of Copyright Protection

Copyright protection extends to expressions and not to ideas, procedures, methods of operation or mathematical concepts as such.

Article 3

Application of Articles 2 to 6 of the Berne Convention Contracting Parties shall apply mutatis mutandis the provisions of Articles 2 to 6 of the Berne Convention in respect of the protection provided for in this Treaty.

Article 4

Computer Programs

Computer programs are protected as literary works within the meaning of Article 2 of the Berne Convention. Such protection applies to computer programs, whatever may be the mode or form of their expression.

Article 5

Compilations of Data (Databases)

Compilations of data or other material, in any form, which by reason of the selection or arrangement of their contents constitute intellectual creations, are protected as such. This protection does not extend to the data or the material itself and is without prejudice to any copyright subsisting in the data or material contained in the compilation.

Article 6

Right of Distribution

(1) Authors of literary and artistic works shall enjoy the exclusive right of authorizing the making available to the public of the original and copies of their works through sale or other transfer of ownership.

(2) Nothing in this Treaty shall affect the freedom of Contracting Parties to determine the conditions, if any, under which the exhaustion of the right in paragraph (1) applies after the first sale or other transfer of ownership of the original or a copy of the work with the authorization of the author.

Article 7

Right of Rental

(1) Authors of: (i) computer programs; (ii) cinematographic works; and (iii) works embodied in phonograms as determined in the national law of Contracting Parties,

shall enjoy the exclusive right of authorizing commercial rental to the public of the originals or copies of their works.

(2) Paragraph (1) shall not apply: (i) in the case of computer programs where the program itself is not the essential object of the rental; and (ii) in the case of cinematographic works, unless such commercial rental has led to widespread copying of such works materially impairing the exclusive right of reproduction.

(3) Notwithstanding the provisions of paragraph (1), a Contracting Party that, on April 15, 1994, had and continues to have in force a system of equitable remuneration of authors for the rental of copies of their works embodied in phonograms may maintain that system provided that the commercial rental of works embodied in phonograms is not giving rise to the material impairment of the exclusive rights of reproduction of authors.

Article 8

Right of Communication to the Public

Without prejudice to the provisions of Articles 11(1)(ii), 11bis(1)(i) and (ii), 11ter(1)(ii), 14(1)(ii) and 14bis(1) of the Berne Convention, authors of literary and artistic works shall enjoy the exclusive right of authorizing any communication to the public of their works, by wire or wireless means, including the making available to the public of their works in such a way that members of the public may access these works from a place and at a time individually chosen by them.

Article 9

Duration of the Protection of Photographic Works In respect of photographic works, the Contracting Parties shall not apply the provisions of Article 7(4) of the Berne Convention.

Article 10

Limitations and Exceptions

(1) Contracting Parties may, in their national legislation, provide for limitations of or exceptions to the rights granted to authors of literary and artistic works under this Treaty in certain special cases that do not conflict with a normal exploitation of the work and do not unreasonably prejudice the legitimate interests of the author.

(2) Contracting Parties shall, when applying the Berne Convention, confine any limitations of or exceptions to rights provided for therein to certain special cases that do not conflict with a normal exploitation of the work and do not unreasonably prejudice the legitimate interests of the author.

Article 11

Obligations concerning Technological Measures

Contracting Parties shall provide adequate legal protection and effective legal remedies against the circumvention of effective technological measures that are used by authors in connection with the exercise of their rights under this Treaty or the Berne Convention and that restrict acts, in respect of their works, which are not authorized by the authors concerned or permitted by law.

Article 12

Obligations concerning Rights Management Information

(1) Contracting Parties shall provide adequate and effective legal remedies against any person knowingly performing any of the following acts knowing or, with respect to civil remedies having reasonable grounds to know, that it will induce, enable, facilitate or conceal an infringement of any right covered by this Treaty or the Berne Convention:

(i) to remove or alter any electronic rights management information without authority;

(ii) to distribute, import for distribution, broadcast or communicate to the public, without authority, works or copies of works knowing that electronic rights management information has been removed or altered without authority.

(2) As used in this Article, "rights management information" means information which identifies the work, the author of the work, the owner of any right in the work, or information about the terms and conditions of use of the work, and any numbers or codes that represent such information, when any of these items of information is attached to a copy of a work or appears in connection with the communication of a work to the public.

Article 13

Application in Time

Contracting Parties shall apply the provisions of Article 18 of the
Berne Convention to all protection provided for in this Treaty.
Article 14

Provisions on Enforcement of Rights

(1) Contracting Parties undertake to adopt, in accordance with their legal systems, the measures necessary to ensure the application of this Treaty.

(2) Contracting Parties shall ensure that enforcement procedures are available under their law so as to permit effective action against any act of infringement of rights covered by this Treaty, including expeditious remedies to prevent

infringements and remedies which constitute a deterrent to further infringements.

Article 15

Assembly

(1) (a) The Contracting Parties shall have an Assembly.

(b) Each Contracting Party shall be represented by one delegate who may be assisted by alternate delegates, advisors and experts.

(c) The expenses of each delegation shall be borne by the Contracting Party that has appointed the delegation. The Assembly may ask the World Intellectual Property Organization (hereinafter referred to as "WIPO") to grant financial assistance to facilitate the participation of delegations of Contracting Parties that are regarded as developing countries in conformity with the established practice of the General Assembly of the United Nations or that are countries in transition to a market economy.

(2) (a) The Assembly shall deal with matters concerning the maintenance and development of this Treaty and the application and operation of this Treaty.

(b) The Assembly shall perform the function allocated to it under Article 17(2) in respect of the admission of certain intergovernmental organizations to become party to this Treaty.

(c) The Assembly shall decide the convocation of any diplomatic conference for the revision of this Treaty and give the necessary instructions to the Director General of WIPO for the preparation of such diplomatic conference.

(3) (a) Each Contracting Party that is a State shall have one vote and shall vote only in its own name.

(b) Any Contracting Party that is an intergovernmental organization may participate in the vote, in place of its Member States, with a number of votes equal to the number of its Member States which are party to this Treaty. No such intergovernmental organization shall participate in the vote if any one of its Member States exercises its right to vote and vice versa.

(4) The Assembly shall meet in ordinary session once every two years upon convocation by the Director General of WIPO.

(5) The Assembly shall establish its own rules of procedure, including the convocation of extraordinary sessions, the requirements of a quorum and, subject to the provisions of this Treaty, the required majority for various kinds of decisions.

Article 16

International Bureau

The International Bureau of WIPO shall perform the administrative tasks concerning the Treaty.

Article 17

Eligibility for Becoming Party to the Treaty

(1) Any Member State of WIPO may become party to this Treaty.

(2) The Assembly may decide to admit any intergovernmental organization to become party to this Treaty which declares that it is competent in respect of, and has its own legislation binding on all its Member States on, matters covered by this Treaty and that it has been duly authorized, in accordance with its internal procedures, to become party to this Treaty.

(3) The European Community, having made the declaration referred to in the preceding paragraph in the Diplomatic Conference that has adopted this Treaty, may become party to this Treaty.

Article 18

Rights and Obligations under the Treaty

Subject to any specific provisions to the contrary in this Treaty, each Contracting Party shall enjoy all of the rights and assume all of the obligations under this Treaty.

Article 19

Signature of the Treaty

This Treaty shall be open for signature until December 31, 1997, by any

Member State of WIPO and by the European Community.
Article 20

Entry into Force of the Treaty

This Treaty shall enter into force three months after 30 instruments of ratification or accession by States have been deposited with the Director General of WIPO.

Article 21

Effective Date of Becoming Party to the Treaty

This Treaty shall bind

(i) the 30 States referred to in Article 20, from the date on which this Treaty has entered into force;

(ii) each other State from the expiration of three months from the date on which the State has deposited its instrument with the Director General of WIPO;

(iii) the European Community, from the expiration of three months after the deposit of its instrument of ratification or accession if such instrument has been deposited after the entry into force of this Treaty according to Article 20, or, three months after the entry into force of this Treaty if such instrument has been deposited before the entry into force of this Treaty;

(iv) any other intergovernmental organization that is admitted to become party to this Treaty, from the expiration of three months after the deposit of its instrument of accession.

Article 22

No Reservations to the Treaty

No reservation to this Treaty shall be admitted.

Article 23

Denunciation of the Treaty

This Treaty may be denounced by any Contracting Party by notification addressed to the Director General of WIPO. Any denunciation shall take effect one year from the date on which the Director General of WIPO received the notification.

Article 24

Languages of the Treaty

(1) This Treaty is signed in a single original in English, Arabic, Chinese, French, Russian and Spanish languages, the versions in all these languages being equally authentic.

(2) An official text in any language other than those referred to in paragraph (1) shall be established by the Director General of WIPO on the request of an interested party, after consultation with all the interested parties. For the purposes of this paragraph, "interested party" means any Member State of WIPO whose official language, or one of whose official languages, is involved and the European Community, and any other intergovernmental organization that may become party to this Treaty, if one of its official languages is involved.

Article 25

Depositary

The Director General of WIPO is the depositary of this Treaty.

U.S. Copyright Office

Note from the Editor.

Odin's Library Classics strives to bring you unedited and unabridged works of classical literature. As such this is the complete and unabridged version of the original. The English language has evolved since the writing and some of the words appear in their original form, or at least the form most commonly used at the time. This is done to protect the original intent of the author. If at any time you are unsure of the meaning of the original meaning of a word, please do your research on that word. It is important to preserve the history of the English language.

Taylor Anderson